Gabler Theses

T0384383

In der Schriftenreihe „Gabler Theses" erscheinen ausgewählte, englischsprachige Doktorarbeiten, die an renommierten Hochschulen in Deutschland, Österreich und der Schweiz entstanden sind. Die Arbeiten behandeln aktuelle Themen der Wirtschaftswissenschaften und vermitteln innovative Beiträge für Wissenschaft und Praxis. Informationen zum Einreichungsvorgang und eine Übersicht unserer Publikationsangebote finden Sie hier.

Weitere Bände in der Reihe https://link.springer.com/bookseries/16768

Lisa Stoll

Providing a New Perspective on Understanding and Measuring of Customer Inspiration

 Springer Gabler

Lisa Stoll
München, Germany

Dissertation Universität München

D19

ISSN 2731-3220   ISSN 2731-3239   (electronic)
Gabler Theses
ISBN 978-3-658-35893-8   ISBN 978-3-658-35894-5   (eBook)
https://doi.org/10.1007/978-3-658-35894-5

Responsible Editor: Marija Kojic
This Springer Gabler imprint is published by the registered company Springer Fachmedien
Wiesbaden GmbH part of Springer Nature.
The registered company address is: Abraham-Lincoln-Str. 46, 65189 Wiesbaden, Germany

Danksagung

Diese Arbeit entstand im Rahmen meiner Tätigkeit als wissenschaftliche Mitarbeiterin am Institut für Marktorientierte Unternehmensführung der Ludwig-Maximilians-Universität München. In dieser Zeit habe ich von vielen Seiten Unterstützung erfahren, für die ich mich bedanken möchte.

Zuallererst möchte ich mich bei meinem Doktorvater Prof. Dr. Manfred Schwaiger bedanken, der mich mit seiner scharfsinnigen Denkweise sehr geprägt hat, sodass die Arbeit an seinem Institut sehr bereichernd war. Durch sein Vertrauen in mich und meine Arbeit sowie seine Unterstützung und anregende Kritik konnte diese Arbeit erst entstehen. Prof. Dr. Anton Meyer danke ich für die Übernahme des Korreferats sowie seine wertvollen Anregungen.

Beim gesamten Institutsteam bedanke ich mich für die gute Zusammenarbeit und spannenden Diskussionen, kurzweiligen Kaffeepausen und geistreichen Gespräche. Ganz besonderes danke ich Marion Pair für ihre Unterstützung im Institutsalltag, aber auch für die vielen privaten Gespräche und die daraus entstandene Freundschaft. Auch Niels Hitz, Johannes Hirschvogel, Maximilian Niederberger-Kern, Chris-Daniel Krempls und Louisa Weritz gilt mein Dank für die vielen unvergesslichen kleinen und großen Momente, die ich mit ihnen erleben durfte. Danke auch an die IMM-Hiwis für ihre tatkräftige Unterstützung.

Bedanken möchte ich mich auch bei meinen Interviewpartnern aus der Praxis, die sich die Zeit genommen haben, meinem Vorhaben zu widmen und meine Fragen zu beantworten, sodass das Fundament dieser Arbeit gelegt werden konnte.

Auch im privaten Umfeld begleiteten mich Menschen, für deren Unterstützung ich sehr dankbar bin. Meinem besten Freund, Thomas Höß, danke ich, dass er immer für mich da war und mich stets motiviert hat. Katja Apalkova danke ich für den kreativen Austausch während etlicher Spaziergänge. Bei Sven, Alex,

Maki und Hans bedanke ich mich für ihre Gastfreundschaft im Pimpernel, dessen Besuch eine willkommene Abwechslung nach intensiven Schreibphasen war. Meinen Eltern sowie meinem Bruder Simon danke ich für ihre Geduld. Und ganz besonders gilt mein Dank meinen beiden Katzen, Ted und Rosa, die im pandemiebedingten Homeoffice stets für Aufheiterung sorgten.

München
September 2021

Introduction

"When I needed inspiration on the presidential campaign, I often turned to music.

It was rap that got my head in the right place."

– Barack Obama–

There are certain moments in life when people are seeking inspiration. Barack Obama did so when he developed his presidential campaign in 2008 (Obama, 2020). Already in ancient Greece, poets asked for inspiration, symbolized by the Muses that were asked for their divine assistance during the writing process (Murray, 1981). Since then, inspiration has been associated with "a higher power" (Clark, 1997, p. 3) and "spiritual influence" (Eliade & Adams, 1987, p. 256), which "evokes creative products or ideas" (Hymer, 1990, p. 17). In the case of the 44th president of the United States, it was rap "that got [his] (my) head in the right place" (Clarke, 2020). It seems that companies also try to get the heads of their customers in the right place nowadays. Indeed, at least, that is what their offerings suggest when companies dedicate entire landing pages to *inspiration* (e.g. Ikea, 2020; Siemens Home, 2020; Tassimo, 2020). Some business models are even grounded on the idea of inspiring consumers (e.g. Pinterest, 2020) or they publish a magazine named after it ("Aldi inspiriert", Aldi Sued, 2020). Inspiration pops up everywhere in marketing communication and the question arises why so many companies talk about inspiration. Is inspiring customers a legitimate driver for brands' and companies' success?

The exploration of inspiration from a scientific perspective is not easy. Due to its divine and spiritual past, the phenomenon appears mysteriously and unscientifically, although psychologists have attempted to uncover inspiration against all odds. Inspiration is a psychological state that involves "evocation, motivation and transcendence" (Thrash & Elliot, 2003, p. 872) and it is characterized by a shift in energy, clarity, openness and connection (Hart, 1998). The state of inspiration enables the actualization of creative ideas, and it can predict the creativity of ideas (Thrash, Maruskin, Cassidy, Fryer, & Ryan, 2010). Writers can profit from inspiration as it is associated with efficiency, productivity, and the use of shorter words (Thrash, Maruskin, et al., 2010). However, not only writers can benefit from inspiration, as it also enhances general well-being for the inspirational experiencer (Thrash, Elliot, Maruskin, & Cassidy, 2010). Even advertisers can benefit, since ads that evoke inspiration are more likely to go viral (Tellis, MacInnis, Tirunillai, & Zhang, 2019).

In fact, marketing scholars have also become interested in the topic and started to uncover customers' inspiration in the marketing domain (e.g. Böttger, Rudolph, Evanschitzky, & Pfrang, 2017; Rudolph, Böttger, & Pfrang, 2012). Their studies provide first evidence that the state of customer inspiration drives emotional, attitudinal and behavioral outcomes like positive affect, customer satisfaction, and impulse buying (Böttger et al., 2017). Whether customers who are inspired also account for a company's long-term success still needs to be investigated. However, we already know that brands that manage to build close relationship-like connections with their customers are able to build a loyal customer base (Khamitov, Wang, & Thomson, 2019). These relationships include brand love (Batra, Ahuvia, & Bagozzi, 2012), self-brand connection (Escalas, 2004) and brand attachment (Park, MacInnis, Priester, Eisingerich, & Iacobucci, 2010). Already since the 1990s, marketing has relied on relationships, which—grounded in trust and commitment—are needed to create long-term relationships with customers (R. Morgan & Hunt, 1994). These long-term relationships seem to be important more than ever, since many markets and brands are under pressure.

In 2020, the COVID-19 pandemic changed consumer needs almost overnight (Campbell, Inman, Kirmani, & Price, 2020; Galoni, Carpenter, & Rao, 2020). Some industries like the tourism or fashion industry were hit especially hard, as travel was suddenly no longer possible and new clothes were no longer necessary during lockdown (Bianchi et al., 2020; Needham, 2020). Within a few weeks, entire demand markets had collapsed and companies had to rethink established concepts to adapt to the new conditions (Luckwaldt, 2020). However, even before the global pandemic crisis, many companies were challenged to gain awareness among their target segment. The overwhelming information and advertising overload that consumers face impede gain a fair share of attention (Ansari & Mela, 2003). Nonetheless, brand awareness is still a prerequisite before consumers can eventually be converted into loyal customers (Bruce, Becker, & Reinartz, 2020).

In addition, our hyperconnected world characterized by "networks of people, devices, and other entities that are continuously interacting and exchanging information" has led to major challenges for brands (Swaminathan, Sorescu, Steenkamp, O'Guinn, & Schmitt, 2020, p. 26). What used to be important for brands has suddenly vanished. According to literature, brands have two main functions (Fischer, Völckner, & Sattler, 2010): first, brands reduce the risk of making a purchase mistake as they suggest a certain product quality (Kapferer, 2008; Nelson, 1970); and second, brands are symbolic devices that allow consumers to communicate about themselves (Levy, 1959) and consequently provide a social demonstrance function towards others (Fischer et al., 2010). These benefits allow companies to charge a significant price premium for certain brands (Fischer et al., 2010). Nonetheless, both functions are becoming less important. For a long time, the signaling effect of brands was justified by the high search costs and the asymmetry of information on the consumer side (Erdem & Swait, 1998). However, brands as a quality signal are no longer important, since consumers are now enabled to constantly access information at a low cost due to technological progress. Additionally, connected consumers and social networks reduce the remaining information asymmetry, which has led to highly-informed consumers (Swaminathan et al., 2020). The symbolic function of brands is also endangered due to hyperconnectivity. In online communities, brands are affected by social influence and they are no longer in single ownership. Brands that are collectively shaped in brand publics (Arvidsson & Caliandro, 2016) are shifted into an environment characterized by "cocreated brand experiences and brand meaning" (Swaminathan et al., 2020, p. 25).

Given that both main functions of brands are affected through our digitalized world, brands need to deliver additional benefits to sacrifice their price premium. This additional benefit might be delivered through the inspiration of customers. The management consulting company BCG creates a scenario for fashion brands in which higher preferences are predicted for either lower-priced goods or premium brands that deliver additional value, serving the higher demand for sustainable and purposeful brands and relevant messages (Bianchi et al., 2020). Customer inspiration which puts the head of customers in the right place could be this key feature for the future success of brands. The first evidence is provided by the agency Prophet, which states that the inspiration of consumers is one of four key factors to become a relevant brand for consumers (Prophet, 2019). However, literature about customer inspiration is still scarce to prove this third proposed function of brands.

This dissertation aims to advance the research about inspiration in marketing by dedicating three consecutive studies to this topic. First, I define and conceptualize customer inspiration within the marketing domain. Second, I develop a measurement tool that helps to assess customer inspiration in an actionable way. Third, I place customer inspiration in relation to other constructs in terms of conceptual and empirical differentiation, as well as its exploratory power.

Study I—titled "Definition and Conceptualization of Customer Inspiration"— is fully dedicated to exploring the phenomenon of inspiration in the marketing domain. Although *inspiration* is widely used in marketing communication by many firms, the varying usage suggests that there is no uniform understanding. Moreover, the conceptual foundation in marketing science remains thin. I attempt to fill this research gap by defining and conceptualizing customer inspiration by means of expert knowledge. The theories-in-use approach is used to develop marketing theory based on theory holders (Zeithaml et al., 2020). Twelve interviews with marketing managers and chief executive officers from e.g. FMCG companies and branding agencies provide the basis for the final definition of customer inspiration as the level of an individual's identification with and activation through a brand's mindset and actions. It is manifested cognitively, affectively and behaviorally through e.g. "aha" experiences, feelings, insights, and the activation of current or potential consumers. I further differentiate customer inspiration from established constructs like customer engagement, brand love, or brand attitude and provide arguments that customer inspiration adds conceptually to existing research in marketing science.

Study II—titled "Measurement Model of Customer Inspiration"—aims to operationalize customer inspiration and transform the theory developed in Study I into an actionable measurement tool. As existing measures of (customer) inspiration do not meet the construct requirements of the newly-conceptualized customer inspiration, Study II develops a reliable and valid measuring model within a six-step procedure that follows the C-OAR-SE procedure (Rossiter, 2002) and takes into account recommendations by Diamantopoulos and Winklhofer (2001). The overall index development comprises two parts. In part 1, four consecutive steps including a literature review, focus group sessions, a qualitative study, and validation interviews help to develop the measurement model by focusing on content validity of the construct. In part 2, the measurement model is validated by means of two empirical studies to reduce and refine the index, as well as assessing its external validity. These steps lead to the specification of customer inspiration as a formative second-order construct with three reflective first-order components, namely connection, transformation, and activation. With a nine-item measure, customer inspiration can be assessed for scientific and practical purposes. The customer inspiration index helps to rate portfolio and competitor brands along the three components of customer inspiration.

Study III—titled "The Explanatory Power of Customer Inspiration"—explores the explanatory relevance of customer inspiration in two empirical online studies. As I delineated customer inspiration from other constructs in Study I, empirical proof concerning whether customer inspiration truly adds value in relation to other constructs was still lacking. Study III tries to fill this gap and compares the explanatory power of the newly-conceptualized customer inspiration with brand attitude and customer inspiration defined by Böttger et al. (2017). The results provide evidence that customer inspiration offers value over brand attitude and the existing customer inspiration construct in predicting both a higher willingness to pay a price premium as well as a higher purchase intention. The results indicate that it is worthwhile for practitioners to invest in activities that inspire customers, besides creating a positive attitude towards the brand. In addition, the results demonstrate that the newly developed nine-item measure of customer inspiration has a higher explanatory power compared to the existing customer inspiration scale.

Contents

Study I: Definition and Conceptualization of Customer Inspiration

Abstract

Customer inspiration seems to be a promising factor to attract, engage, and retain customers in a highly competitive market environment. The expression *inspiration* is on everyone's lips within advertising language, although its conceptual foundation in marketing science remains thin and requires further clarification. This study attempts to fill this gap by defining and conceptualizing the construct of customer inspiration with the theories-in-use approach for which expert interviews were conducted. The analysis of the twelve interviews led to the finding that customer inspiration is the level of an individual's identification with and activation through a brand's mindset and actions. It is manifested cognitively, affectively and behaviorally through e.g. "aha" experiences, feelings, insights, and activation of current or potential consumers. Customer inspiration can occur both within and outside of the direct consumer-brand encounter. Customer inspiration comprises three major themes, namely activation, personal insight, and deep connection. A conceptual differentiation from established constructs provides initial evidence that customer inspiration is conceptually distinct from constructs like customer engagement, brand love, or brand attitude.

A previous, merely conceptual version of this article was submitted as a project study for the Master of Business Research (Ludwig-Maximilians-Universität, Munich) in December 2019.

Supplementary Information The online version contains supplementary material available at (https://doi.org/10.1007/978-3-658-35894-5_1).

1.1   Motivation

How to create loyal customers and attach them to a brand to build long-term customer relationships is one of the fundamental topics in marketing science and practice (Keller, 2020; Khamitov et al., 2019). Defined as "a collection of attitudes aligned with a series of purchase behaviors that systematically favor one entity over competing entities" (G. Watson, Beck, Henderson, & Palmatier, 2015, p. 793), customer loyalty represents a desirable goal from the company's perspective. It describes a clear and long-lasting consumer preference for one product or brand over the other. Companies that have achieved a loyal customer base benefit in various ways, such as increased word of mouth (WOM) and better firm performance (G. Watson et al., 2015). The key question is how a company can achieve this privileged situation of having loyal customers and increased retention.

For a long time, retention rate optimization was mainly grounded on product or service refinement, as well as increased marketing investments (Reinartz & Kumar, 2000). This is no longer sufficient to ensure customer retention, capitalization of customers' lifetime value, and long-term competitive advantage (Kumar & Pansari, 2016). Customer-based metrics that place the customer at the center of attention like commitment (Verhoef, 2003), consumer-brand relationships (Fournier, 1998), or customer identification (Ahearne, Bhattacharya, & Gruen, 2005) have grown in importance for organizational performance (Van Doorn et al., 2010). A market environment that has become even more challenging for companies in recent decades due to technological progress reinforces this requirement for customer centricity (Bruhn & Meffert, 2002). Higher market transparency, a faster willingness to switch, price-sensitive customers, and international competition are among the many factors that hinder long-term customer retention (Bruhn & Meffert, 2002). Convincing customers to stick to a brand or company is even more challenging as the customer journey has changed into a much more flexible and volatile process with empowered consumers (Neosperience, 2018). Therefore, it holds particular importance for management and marketing experts to find ways to bind customers.

A promising way to create customer loyalty that has been researched in the last two decades is by investing in customer-brand relationships. This field of study can be traced back to Fournier (1998, p. 343), who analyzed "the relationships consumers form with the brands they know and use". Her work on relationship theory built a framework for evaluating consumer-brand connections and initiated a new research stream with related topics (Fetscherin & Heinrich, 2015). The main work has been conducted around five consumer-brand connection types (Khamitov et al., 2019), namely brand love (Batra et al., 2012), brand attachment (Malär, Krohmer, Hoyer, & Nyffenegger, 2011; Park, Eisingerich, & Park, 2013), self-brand connection (Escalas & Bettman, 2003), brand identification (Stokburger-Sauer, Ratneshwar, & Sen, 2012), and brand trust (Chaudhuri & Holbrook, 2001). All of these constructs explain certain aspects that connect a customer to a brand or company.

Another way of building customer loyalty is by creating relevant brands that inspire consumers (Prophet, 2019). Hence, customer inspiration could involve one aspirant who joins the series of customer-brand relationship constructs. The branding agency Prophet states that "relevant brands engage, surprise, connect", and make a difference in consumers' lives (Prophet, 2019, p. 6). Pinterest (2020) mentions that the beginning of the purchasing process is an especially productive moment to inspire, when the consumer is still in the exploration phase and has not yet committed him-/herself to a brand. Their claim summarizes this as: "On Pinterest, brands inspire—they don't interrupt" (Pinterest, 2020). LEGO Group's key mission is formulated as "Inspire and Develop the Builders of Tomorrow" (Lego, 2020). The mission implies that inspiration lies in the focus of a leading brand in the toys segment. With an annual revenue of 5.2 billion euros (Lego, 2019), LEGO inspires people all around the world, builds emotional connections with the customer and has remained successful over the last 90 years.

Many companies across several industries use expressions like *inspiration, inspiring,* or *inspire* in their marketing activities (e.g., GoPro, 2020; Lego, 2020; Pinterest, 2020; Siemens Home, 2020). Due to the manifold range of its use, it seems to be used as a buzzword rather than a marketing concept with a streamlined direction. This fact does not contradict the relevance of the topic, but rather it shows how important it is to properly define the term and conceptualize customer inspiration and distinguish it from other constructs such as brand love, and brand attachment.

The first attempts have already been made to characterize customer inspiration in marketing literature. Böttger et al. (2017) define customer inspiration as "a customer's temporary motivational state that facilitates the transition from the reception of a marketing-induced idea to the intrinsic pursuit of a consumption-related goal" (Böttger et al., 2017, p. 117). The authors base their definition on Thrash and Elliot (2003), who researched inspiration in psychology. However, the theoretical foundation of Böttger et al. (2017) only takes into account parts of the psychological literature and omits essential work by e.g. Hart (1998). In addition, it is unclear what relationship customer inspiration has with (supposedly) related constructs, such as consumer engagement or brand attachment. This study aims to build on this and tries to answer the following research questions:

RQ1: How should customer inspiration be defined?

RQ2: How can customer inspiration be conceptualized?

RQ3: What is the difference between customer inspiration and other related constructs?

To address the first and second questions, we conducted a qualitative study with expert interviews as the main data source. Using the theories-in-use approach (Zaltman, Lemasters, & Heffring, 1982; Zeithaml et al., 2020), theory was extracted by levering expert knowledge. In order to address the third question of how customer inspiration differs from other constructs, related constructs are conceptually distinguished. In particular, the following constructs are examined: consumer engagement (Brodie, Hollebeek, Jurić, & Ilić, 2011), customer co-creation (Pee, 2016), brand love (Bagozzi, Batra, & Ahuvia, 2017), brand attachment (Malär et al., 2011; Park et al., 2013), and brand attitude (Rossiter, 2014).

The remainder of this study is organized as follows. We first provide the theoretical background of (customer) inspiration from different scientific perspectives to highlight the gaps in the current conceptualization of customer inspiration. We then proceed with an overview of the qualitative study and highlight the results of the theory construction. The extracted findings will be backed up by a literature review. Subsequently, customer inspiration will be compared with and distinguished from other existing constructs. Finally, we conclude with a discussion as well as a brief outlook for further studies.

1.2   Literature Review

The term *inspiration* appears in many studies across a range of disciplines, such as psychology, theology, musicology, management, education, engineering, and anthropology (Eliade & Adams, 1987; Oleynick, Thrash, Lefew, Moldovan, & Kieffaber, 2014; Thrash & Elliot, 2003). A detailed discussion has taken place particularly in literature and psychology (Hart, 1998; Murray, 1981; Thrash & Elliot, 2004). For the purpose of this study, it is first necessary to delve into the roots of inspiration. We start with a theoretical background of inspiration in general and proceed by analyzing its definition and conceptualization in psychological science, before we bridge the topic to the marketing domain.

1.2.1 Inspiration from a General and Psychological Perspective

In the following, we first take a broader perspective on the expression *inspiration* and shed light on descriptions and periphrases in literature and theology, followed by an analysis of several definitions.

Descriptions and Periphrases of Inspiration
The notion *inspiration* has a long history. In the context of aesthetics, it traces back to Plato's *Ion,* when inspiration was equivalent to the Muses, which were "whispering, breathing, or singing into the recipient" (Clark, 1997, p. 1). The Ancient Greek describe inspiration's content to be of "truth, beauty, and goodness" (Hart, 1998, p. 8). From an etymological perspective, inspiration comes from the Latin term *inspirare*, which means "to breathe into, to be filled, to inflame" (Merriam-Webster, 2018). This Latin term in turn initially translated the Greek expression *enthusiasmos* (Clark, 1997, p. 3), which stands for "being taken by a higher power", often being personified with gods (Landfester, 2006). The Oxford English Dictionary (1989, p. 1036) describes inspiration as: "A breathing in or infusion of some idea, purpose, etc. into the mind; the suggestion, awakening, or creation of some feeling or impulse, especially of an exalted kind". Williams (1982, p. 1) states that inspiration is "(…) means of gaining knowledge", "(…) achieving wisdom", and "(…) essential to creativity".

Davitz (1969) interprets inspiration as an emotion and analyzed its meaning by searching for descriptions of this emotional state. He identified eleven items for inspiration based on the recipients' descriptions, e.g. "I am excited in a calm way", "I feel strong inside", "there is an inner buoyancy", "I seem more alert", "more alive", "with a sense of vitality, aliveness, vibrancy, an extra spurt of energy or drive", and "I seem to be functioning intellectually at a higher level" (Davitz, 1969, p. 67).

In the context of literature, inspiration is often associated with a state of higher energy (Bowra, 1955; Murray, 1981), "influence" (Bradley, 1929, p. 225) or "spiritual influence" (Eliade & Adams, 1987, p. 256). Table 1.1 provides an overview of descriptions and periphrases of inspiration.

Table 1.1 Descriptions and periphrases of inspiration

Source	Context	Descriptions & Periphrases of Inspiration
Oxford English Dictionary (1989)	Dictionary	"A breathing in or infusion of some idea, purpose, etc. into the mind; the suggestion, awakening, or creation of some feeling or impulse, especially of an exalted kind." (p. 1036)
Bowra (1955)	Literature	"(…) when we say that a poem is inspired, we mean that it has an unusual degree of power (…)." (p. 20)
Bradley (1929)	Literature	"(…) a peculiar influence on certain persons, issuing in speech or in writing of which they would otherwise be incapable." (p. 225)
Eliade and Adams (1987)	Theology	"(…) a spiritual influence that occurs spontaneously and renders a person capable of thinking, speaking, or acting in ways that transcend ordinary human capacities." (p. 256)
Davitz (1969)	Psychology	"I am exited in a calm way", "I feel strong inside", "there is an inner buoyancy", "I seem more alert", "more alive", "with a sense of vitality, aliveness, vibrancy, an extra spurt of energy or drive", "I seem to be functioning intellectually at a higher level" (p. 67)
Hymer (1990)	Psychology	"Inspiration occurs when an individual establishes an intense object relationship which evokes creative products or ideas which would not otherwise materialize." (p. 17)

Definitions and Conceptualizations of Inspiration.
Some authors have attempted to define inspiration (Table 1.2). In the following, we focus on the most important definitions in terms of the reference of scientific studies.

Hart (1998, p. 12) identified four characteristics that constitute experiences of inspiration, namely "connection, opened, clarity, and energy". Each of the four characteristics is present within an experience of inspiration. *Connection* describes the change in boundaries between the individual who experiences inspiration and the objects of his surroundings. Objects of connection include nature, ideas, other people or the self, depending on the situation where inspiration occurs. For a painter, this object could be his canvas. Through the sensation of connection, the boundaries can be temporarily dissolved. In his studies, Hart (1998) observes that this connection can take place in peak experiences

(Privette, 1983), while it also occurs in everyday situations. The second characteristic of *opened* refers to the state of being receptive or available. Some described this characteristic as "letting go" and "flowed through" (Hart, 1998, p. 15). The consequence of feeling opened was often described as being "filled" by some sort of warmth, light, or energy (Hart, 1998, p. 15). As an example, the author mentions a writer whose writing felt as easy as if he was taking dictation. The source of inspiration—and consequently to what *opened to* relates—is not necessarily "from the outside". Based on Hart (1998, p. 17), it depends on the individual experiencer and his level of consciousness whether it appears as "from the outside" or something from inside. The third characteristic of *clarity* includes phenomena of sensory and cognitive clarity after individuals have experienced the state of connection and openness (Hart, 1998). Sensory clarity comprises transient synesthetic and multi-sensory experiences. The author provides an example of a musician who perceives his work in the form of structures or colors. Cognitive clarity includes an overall understanding, not necessarily intellectually but rather in a way whereby people gain "a larger perspective in life" (Hart, 1998, p. 18). Overall, the "emotional-cognitive network is specific for inspiration" (Hart, 1998, p. 19). The fourth characteristic describes a shift in *energy* of either one's emotional or physical appearance. Hart (1998, p. 19) identified strong emotional shifts of positive valence, which were described by participants as "joy" or "excitement". Physically, people experience inspiration as uplifting, refreshing and energizing. The results of his study prompted him to define inspiration as "a specific epistemic process that provides psychological and spiritual sustenance and is characterized by a remembrance or recognition of some knowledge or perspective valuable in the social or psychological context given" (Hart, 1998, p. 32). According to Hart (1998), inspiration can appear in both form and being. Form can take different shapes, e.g. an idea for a scientific paper or a solution to a problem. The author also found that the described experiences of inspiration did not describe motivation; rather, motivation was an outcome of a somewhat enlightening event.

Thrash and Elliot (2003) distinguish between inspiration from within and above, referring to its different sources. Inspiration from within is defined "as a motivational state that is triggered by a compelling idea or illumination (...) and that is targeted toward the actualization or realization of the idea" (Thrash & Elliot, 2003, p. 872). Inspiration from above is defined as "a motivational state evoked by a revelation (trigger) and directed toward the conversion of transcendent, revealed knowledge into a work of art, a text, or some other concrete form (target)" (Thrash & Elliot, 2003, p. 872). Inspiration from within comes from an intrapsychic source, such as the unconscious, preconscious and the perceptual

Table 1.2 Definitions of inspiration

Source	Context	Definition of Inspiration
Murray (1981)	Literature	"Inspiration can be broadly defined as the temporary impulse to poetic creation, and relates primarily to the poetic process." (p. 89)
Hart (1998)	Psychology	"Inspiration is a specific epistemic process that provides psychological and spiritual sustenance and is characterized by a remembrance or recognition of some knowledge or perspective valuable in the social or psychological context given." (p. 32)
Thrash and Elliot (2003)	Psychology	"Inspiration *from above* as a motivational state evoked by a revelation (trigger) and directed toward the conversion of transcendent, revealed knowledge into a work of art, a text, or some other concrete form (target)." (p. 872)
	Psychology	"Inspiration *from within* may thus be conceptualized as a motivational state that is triggered by a compelling idea or illumination (…) and that is targeted toward the actualization or realization of the idea." (p. 872)
Hymer (1990)	Psychology	"Inspiration occurs when an individual establishes an intense object relationship which evokes creative products or ideas which would not otherwise materialize." (p. 17)

field, whereby inspiration from above derives from environmental sources, like persons or objects. Social comparison theory delivers explanations why people are moved by people who seem e.g. to be superior to themselves (Lockwood & Kunda, 1997).

Both forms are conceptualized as a tripartite construct characterized by "evocation, motivation, and transcendence" (Thrash & Elliot, 2003, p. 885). *Evocation* implies that inspiration occurs spontaneously, unplanned, and out of an unintended situation. Inspiration's emergence is of a rather passive nature without the active search of the recipient for new input. The evocation characteristic underlines the notion that inspiration is neither forced nor pressured and without any responsibility felt to become inspired (Thrash, Elliot, et al., 2010, p. 489). The second characteristic of *motivation* indicates that inspiration involves "the energization and direction of behavior" (Thrash & Elliot, 2003, p. 871). As the third characteristic, *transcendence* describes inspiration's content as being of a supernatural essence. This characteristic is often accompanied by clarity, an awakened mind, and an extended vision (Thrash, Elliot, et al., 2010). Thrash and Elliot (2003) conceptualize inspiration as both a trait and state. While the *state* of inspiration is rather favored by situational emotions, the *trait* of inspiration hints towards pre-existing mindsets.

Within a consecutive study (Thrash & Elliot, 2004), inspiration is conceptualized as a component process with an *inspired-by* and *inspired-to* part. An episode of inspiration comprises both components. The *inspired-by* component considers the intrinsic appreciation of the inspiration stimuli. After being inspired-by something, one's mindset most optimally shifts to a motivational state, while the *inspired-to* component is associated with an appetitive motivation (Thrash & Elliot, 2004). Additional work added the transmission model to the conceptualization of inspiration, which describes the transformation of an antecedent or source (e.g. a creative idea) into an outcome (e.g. a creative product). Inspiration functions as a mediator that facilitates this transformation (Thrash, Maruskin, et al., 2010).

Thrash and Elliot (2003), and Thrash, Maruskin, et al. (2010) have laid a fundamental basis for research on inspiration with the provision of substantial insights into its construct and process. Within several studies, they built the cornerstone for subsequent research about inspiration in psychology (e.g., Rauschnabel, Felix, & Hinsch, 2019; Stephan et al., 2015; Thrash, Maruskin, Moldovan, Oleynick, & Belzak, 2017).

Summary

The preceding elaborations lead to the consolidation that three essential characteristics of inspiration can be identified based on the descriptions and periphrases provided. First, inspiration implies an elevated state of *energy* (Bowra, 1955; Davitz, 1969). Second, inspiration appears as something *passive* and not actively evoked (Eliade & Adams, 1987; Hymer, 1990). Third, inspiration is of high value and perceived as something *special* (Bradley, 1929; Davitz, 1969; Eliade & Adams, 1987). A comparison of the definitions leads to four components that constitute inspiration. First, the essence of inspiration can be described as an *impulse, process,* or *state* (Hart, 1998; Murray, 1981; Thrash & Elliot, 2003), meaning that inspiration is a temporary phenomenon. Second, inspiration is of a *motivational* and *epistemic nature* (Hart, 1998; Thrash & Elliot, 2003). Third, it is something *special* and therefore seen as precious (Hart, 1998; Hymer, 1990; Murray, 1981; Thrash & Elliot, 2003). Fourth, it is triggered by *a revelation, idea* or *illumination* (Thrash & Elliot, 2003). Within the tripartite conceptualization,

Thrash and Elliot (2003) make reference to three of the characteristics by Hart (1998), namely *clarity* (as part of transcendence), *energy* (as part of motivation), and *opened* (as part of evocation). This consolidation shows that the authors complement each other in their examination of inspiration. Inspiration is a temporary phenomenon that is characterized by a shift in energy and a moment of openness, clarity, and connection. Its motivational and epistemic nature suddenly appears, triggered by a revelation, idea, or illumination.

1.2.2 Inspiration from a Marketing Perspective

Customer inspiration is quite a new topic within marketing literature, grounded mainly on the work by Böttger et al. (2017) as well as related previous publications by the authors (Böttger, 2015; Rudolph et al., 2012; Rudolph, Böttger, Pfrang, & Evanschitzky, 2015). Studies relating to their work have since been published regularly (e.g., Balabanis & Chatzopoulou, 2019; Rauschnabel et al., 2019).

The construct is defined as "a cognitive and motivational state that is evoked by marketing stimuli, incorporates the realization of new or enhanced consumption-related insights, and motivates customers to purchase a product or service" (Rudolph et al., 2015, p. 25). Other scholars define customer inspiration as "a customer's temporary motivational state that facilitates the transition from the reception of a marketing-induced idea to the intrinsic pursuit of a consumption-related goal" (Böttger et al., 2017, p. 117).

Similar to the psychological construct by Thrash and Elliot (2004), customer inspiration is conceptualized with an *inspired-by* and an *inspired-to* component (Böttger et al., 2017). *Inspired-by* represents the activation state caused by an external marketing stimulus. The customer feels the urge to implement a new idea or buy a product, before moving from the activation state to the intention state, represented by the *inspired-to* component in which inspiration leads to the motivation to actualize an idea. The two components are linked as the *inspired-by* component mediates the effect of an external stimulus on the *inspired-to* component (Böttger et al., 2017). *Inspired-by* shows stronger correlations with antecedents of inspiration, while *inspired-to* shows stronger correlations with consequences of inspiration (Rudolph et al., 2015). Customer inspiration is conceptualized as a second-order construct with two first-order components (*inspired-by* and *inspired-to*) (Böttger et al., 2017). A graphic of their framework can be seen in Appendix 1 within the Electronic Supplementary Material.

1.2.3 Summary of Literature Review

The history of inspiration dates way back to the Ancient Greeks. Many disciplines have dealt with inspiration, such as theology, musicology, management, education, engineering, and anthropology. Psychology in particular has defined and conceptualized the construct. More recently, the topic has been picked up by marketing scholars. Existing work of customer inspiration within the marketing domain (Böttger et al., 2017) shares similarities with inspiration defined by Thrash and Elliot (2003), which can be seen in the definitions.

> Definition of customer inspiration (Böttger et al., 2017, p. 129): "Customer inspiration [is] (as) a customer's temporary motivational state that facilitates the transition from the reception of a marketing-induced idea to the intrinsic pursuit of a consumption-related goal."

> Definition of inspiration (Thrash & Elliot, 2003, p. 872): "Inspiration from within (may thus) [is] (be conceptualized as) a motivational state that is triggered by a compelling idea or illumination (...) and that is targeted toward the actualization or realization of the idea."

Böttger et al. (2017) explicitly cite the consistency with different literature streams as an advantage and follow the call to contextualize inspiration for specific domains (Thrash & Elliot, 2004). For both, (customer) inspiration is a temporary state of an individual triggered by a stimulus that leads to an activation to take an action. Both authors mention the work by Hart (1998) within their conceptual foundation of each conceptualization, but connection, opened, clarity, and energy are mostly neglected afterwards in the definition, conceptualization, or measurement instrument.

Two shortcomings of the work on customer inspiration can be identified. First, Böttger et al. (2017) mostly borrow from the psychological domain to derive the conceptualization of customer inspiration but let only parts of the psychological literature flow into their work, which could lead to a biased result. Second, borrowing from other disciplines can restrict theory construction to things that are already known. The full potential of exploring the overall phenomenon is not fully leveraged (Zeithaml et al., 2020). We want to address these two points with our study. The first point has just been addressed by a thorough literature review, whereas the second point will be addressed in a qualitative study using the theories-in-use approach (Zeithaml et al., 2020). We conducted twelve interviews with experts from marketing and management. By analyzing their perspective of customer inspiration, we derive a conceptualization grounded in the marketing context. The details of this study are described in the next chapter.

1.3   A Qualitative Study to Define Customer Inspiration

1.3.1 Methodology

A qualitative study was conducted following the grounded theory method (Glaser & Strauss, 1967). The data was gathered from expert interviews to identify theories-in-use (Zaltman et al., 1982). This approach supports the conceptualization process by delivering data based on experts and theory holders. It leads to organic marketing theory, which is based on constructs uniquely grounded in the specific marketing context rather than borrowing theory from other disciplines. The benefit is that thoughts and ideas are less restricted than in the borrowing condition since they are not biased from previews research (Zeithaml et al., 2020). The rationale behind the theories-in-use approach is that "knowledge (…) is the mapping of experienced reality" (Zaltman et al., 1982, p. 118). We used this approach because it enables theory construction from the real, "behavioral" world that guides to a relevant outcome for both managers and marketing scientists. Since the basis of the theories-in-use approach lies within the analysis of expert knowledge, interviews with marketing and management experts were conducted. The outcome of this qualitative study is the theory of customer inspiration organically built within the discipline.

1.3.2 Sampling and Data Collection

In order to identify real experts (i.e. theory holders) in the field of customer inspiration, a mix of different sampling techniques was applied. First, a pool of relevant companies that explicitly used the expression *inspiration* within the visible marketing communication of a company was created. We further selected other companies from various industries that did not explicitly use the term *inspiration* in their marketing activities but advertise extensively towards consumers. Second, it was necessary to identify real people as the actual theory holders who have had decision power within one of the identified companies and were still connected to the operational work. Ideally, these theory holders were either chief marketing officers (or equivalent) or responsible for brand and marketing communication. The position strongly depended on the company size and structure. This two-step-approach provided a pool of potential interview candidates and set the base for the sampling procedure.

Within the theoretical sampling approach, the data is constantly analyzed during the data collection process (Flick, 2007). The interview participants are successively selected within each phase based on the progress of theory construction (Zeithaml et al., 2020). This sampling approach fits research processes where theory is built on multiple theory holders (Johnson & Sohi, 2016). Strauss and Corbin (1990, p. 177) describe it as "sampling on the basis of concepts that have proven theoretical relevance to the evolving theory". In other words, the sampling decision is based on the collected and analyzed data and in an ongoing process.

The interviews took place via telephone. All interviews were recorded with a voice recorder and transcribed afterwards. The interviews followed a semi-structured approach with a set of fixed questions and follow-up questions dependent on the conversation flow. Depending on the stage of theory construction, the questions slightly changed. At the beginning, the questions focused more on the concept development, whereas at a later stage the questions focused more on checking the boundaries of the construct and extracting propositions like antecedents and consequences, as well as moderator variables (Zeithaml et al., 2020). Table 1.3 provides an overview of the core questions within each of the three stages.

Table 1.3   Key questions of expert interviews within each phase (based on Zeithaml et al., 2020)

Phase	Key Objective	Key Questions
Early Stage	Gaining a broad overview of the topic	What importance does inspiration have for you in marketing? What does it mean for you to inspire customers? How is it different from other marketing communication? What stays if we take inspiration away from marketing communication?
Middle Stage	Reinforcing the construct meaning	What importance does inspiration have for you in marketing? What does it mean for you to inspire customers? Based on other interviews, I found out that customer inspiration is about … Would you agree?
Finale Stage	Building if-then propositions	What importance does inspiration have for you in marketing? What does it mean for you to inspire customers? What do you do to inspire customers? Under which conditions works it best to inspire customers?

We interviewed twelve experts that were all professionals in marketing and/or had a managerial position with a clear marketing background. Four of them were female (33.3%). Six of them worked in a consulting & agency cluster (50%), the rest within a corporation (50%). The interviews lasted 25 minutes, on average. Demographics and background information appear in Table 1.4.

Table 1.4 Demographics and information on interview participants

R	Age	Position	Department	Industry	Employees	Cluster
1	43	Customer Service Expert & Author	Self-employed	Consulting	21–50	Consulting & Agency
2	34	Communication Manager	Marketing	Furniture & Interior Design	51–200	Corporation
3	45	CEO	Management & Marketing	Cosmetics	1,001–5,000	Corporation
4	49	CEO & Co-Founder	Marketing & Strategy	Media & Advertising	1–20	Consulting & Agency
5	39	Head of Digital Marketing, GER	Marketing & Strategy	Tobacco	>50,000	Corporation
6	25	CEO & Co-Founder	Management & Marketing	Fashion	1–20	Corporation
7	52	CEO & Co-Founder	Marketing	Media & Advertising	1–20	Consulting & Agency
8	45	CEO & Co-Founder	Management & Marketing	Media & Advertising	21–50	Consulting & Agency
9	38	CEO & Founder	Management	Tourism	1–20	Consulting
10	41	CEO & Co-Founder	Management	IT	1–20	Corporation
11	40	Account Director	Marketing	Media & Advertising	1,001–5,000	Consulting & Agency
12	37	CEO	Management	Interior Design	201–1000	Corporation

Note: R = Respondent

1.3.3 Data Analysis

The main objectives of the data analysis of qualitative interviews are to consolidate and prepare the data to obtain an outcome of condensed form. By shortening and generalizing what has been said, the transformation from qualitative interviews into theory took place (Flick, 2007). We used several methods to analyze the data and extract the key messages from each interview. Besides classic techniques such as text analysis of the transcribed interviews as well as open, selective and axial coding (Flick, 2007), we also created schematic sketches for each interview to graphically illustrate the results and identify common shapes among the sketches afterwards. Two additional independent student researchers analyzed the sketches to arrive at an independent assessment of the results. We identified three themes that constitute customer inspiration, which are presented in the next chapter.

1.4   Results

1.4.1 Overview

This chapter presents an overview of the main outcomes of the qualitative study. It contains the definition of customer inspiration, three main themes, and the overall conceptual framework of customer inspiration. The chapter concludes with a differentiation of customer inspiration from other well-established constructs.

The definition of customer inspiration was derived with a bottom-up approach where the first identified themes built the base for the conceptualization and definition (Sabatier, 1986). We applied a similar approach as Linda Hollebeek (2011b). Each theme is grounded in the expert interviews as well as existing literature. A theoretical foundation that helped to support the theory and findings was added afterwards. We combine the two steps in the following chapter for each theme to avoid duplications, and we added statements from the experts as references. The post-hoc theoretical foundation followed the logic of the grounded theory approach, where researchers should explore a new topic in the most unbiased manner possible (Glaser & Strauss, 1967). The conceptual framework summarizes the definition of customer inspiration and its themes but adds other findings from the expert interviews that help to conceptualize the broader nomological network of customer inspiration with its drivers and outcomes. Since these outcomes—although grounded in expert interviews—have some sort of a speculative character, these outcomes are provided in the form of propositions. At the end, customer inspiration is differentiated from other constructs. By defining the scope of the construct and demonstrating its boundaries, we set the domain of customer inspiration (Brodie, Hollebeek, Jurić, & Ilić, 2011; Jarvis, Mackenzie, Podsakoff, Mick, & Bearden, 2003).

1.4.2 Customer Inspiration Definition

The analysis of the transcribed interviews revealed common themes of customer inspiration that helped to develop the following definition of customer inspiration.

Customer inspiration is defined as the level of an individual's identification with and activation through a brand's mindset and actions. The individuals can be current or potential consumers. Customer inspiration is manifested cognitively, affectively, and behaviorally. The cognitive and affective elements of customer inspiration incorporate e.g. "aha" experiences, feelings, and insights of customers, and the behavioral element captures the activation of current or potential consumers both within and outside of the direct consumer-brand encounter. Customer inspiration involves a deep connection that individuals form with organizations, based on their personal experiences with the mindset and actions of a brand. Potential or current customers build authenticity-based relationships through intense identification with the brand, based on the unique connection that they have with the brand.

This definition follows a similar structure as Vivek, Beatty, and Morgan (2012), who defined customer engagement, whereby the two constructs will be placed into relation in section 1.4.5. Before doing so, customer inspiration and its distinct themes will be discussed in more detail, with the help of quotes from the expert interviews.

1.4.3 Key Customer Inspiration Themes

1.4.3.1 Activation

The respondents' statements in Table 1.5 reveal that for many experts inspiration includes "activating" customers. One respondent said "when you inspire people, you are asking them to take action" (R1). Other descriptions include "inspire to improve" (R5), "activating in a sense of action" (R5), "to initiate their ideas, to project associations, feelings, thoughts" (R7), and "inspire them to act" (R8). We summarized these statements under the theme *activation*.

Similarly, Hart (1998) mentions a shift in energy level as one characteristic of inspiration. This energy was "occasionally translated into immediate action" (Hart, 1998, p. 20). Within the respondents' statements, we identified two forms of activation that inspiration evokes. First, it can take the form of a real action as a behavior towards the brand or beyond, described as being "inspired to do something" (R5), "inspire to act" (R8), or "that they actually do something" (R8). Second, inspiration can also activate cognition, which was described as being "inspired to think about something" and "initiate their ideas". The activation in a form of real behavior also appears in the descriptions of the construct of consumer engagement (e.g., Van Doorn et al., 2010; Vivek et al., 2012). However, through inspiration, activated behavior is not limited to the interaction with the brand as a service relationship, which is the case for consumer engagement (Yu, Patterson, & de Ruyter, 2015). It can also take form outside of the consumer-brand encounter; for instance, as taking action towards "the individual purpose" (R10). The statements also reveal that the activation is caused by the brand. One expert mentioned that activation takes place through a company's or brand's "own behavior" (R1). The organization or brand operates like a role model that transforms the customer with its own behavior.

Organizations or brands that have the ability to move consumers can be compared with charismatic leaders. Charismatic leadership theory is part of management and organizational science. Besides "charismatic" leadership, the leadership style is often also described as "transformational", "visionary", or even "inspirational" (Howell & Shamir, 2005, p. 98). Although some differentiate between charismatic and transformational leadership (Avolio & Yammarino, 2013), we use the two terms synonymously. Charismatic leaders are described as "exceptional leaders who have extraordinary effects on their followers and eventually on social systems. (…) Such leaders transform the needs, values, preferences and aspirations of followers from self-interest to collective interests" (Shamir, House, & Arthur, 1993, p. 577). The parties involved are the leader with exceptional qualities, and followers with "certain perceptions, emotions and attitudes toward the leader" (Howell & Shamir, 2005, p. 98). Yukl (1998, p. 6) defines the follower as "a person who acknowledges the focal leader as a continuing source of guidance and inspiration, regardless of whether there is any formal reporting relationship". The base for such a charismatic relationship is the strong connection between the follower's self-concepts and the leader or the collective mission (Howell & Shamir, 2005). Within a charismatic relationship, followers can identify with the leader or collective mission and see the relationship as a way to express aspects of their self-concepts (ib.). Charismatic leadership refers to an interpersonal relationship and it cannot be directly transferred to the consumer-brand relationship context. Given that consumers can form human-like relationships with brands (Fournier, 1998), for customer inspiration it might be the case that brands are perceived as charismatic leaders that offer direction.

Apart from real action, activation also refers to behavioral intention or motivation (Ajzen, 1985) and the cognitive imagination of a certain situation (e.g. an experience in the customer's mind) (Weisberg, 2014).

Table 1.5 Illustrative respondent statements for the "activation" dimension

- *"When you inspire people, you are asking them to take action through your own behaviors. Might be through the way you are communicating or talking or the way you are behaving or acting. It is inspiring someone to act, to take action" (R1).*
- *"We love to work creatively and want to encourage our customers to do so through our interactive events" (R2, translated from German).*
- *"[...] At the core it's to inspire other people or to change yourself somehow, to improve" (R5, translated from German).*
- *"[...] Inspiration a) is emotional and b) activating in the sense of action, so I am inspired to do something or I am inspired to think about something or I am inspired to find something good or to change something but inspiration has the highest value of all" (R5, translated from German).*
- *"Inspiration means to bring people to something that they have not thought of before. To initiate their ideas, to project associations, feelings, thoughts into their brain windings" (R7, translated from German).*
- *"So we want to get people to action and inspire them to act, but we also want them to feel something inside, so inspired is a lot. [...] What I am talking about is trying to make people feel something emotionally, so that they are inspired to act. That they actually do something, because they feel it" (R8).*
- *"Because our social purpose marketing is all about conveying information and activating, addressing and inspiring the individual's purpose and arousing emotions" (R10).*

1.4.3.2 Personal Insight

The respondent statements in Table 1.6 suggest that customer inspiration includes a moment of "transformation" (R1). One respondent said that in order to inspire customers, brands or organizations need to "change their mindset" (R6). Other descriptions include "to encourage our customers" (R2), to communicate in a "meaningful" way (R3) and inspiration through "purpose" (R3). We summarize these quotes under the theme of *personal insight*.

This theme reflects a cognitive component of customer inspiration that can occur in different forms. Similarly to the *opened* characteristic of Hart (1998), inspiration triggers new thoughts or ideas. As one expert from an apparel online shop said: "We want to help (…) [customers] to change their mindset and offer them beautiful alternatives through our concept, such as how they can consume better, what they have to pay attention to when they buy a garment" (R6). The company seems to not only sell clothes but it also educates the customer indirectly with its own concept. Inspiration further opens a customer's mindset by stimulating his/her thoughts. One respondent mentioned: "We love creativity and want to encourage our customers to design their homes creatively and according to their own wishes and needs" (R2). Inspiring brands can trigger thoughts that have a transformative character, similarly to a charismatic leader (Conger & Kanungo, 1987). One expert mentioned that customers "want relationships that deeply connect them with some sort of transformation, some sort of growth" (R1).

Personal insight contains the term *personal*, which suggests that the transformational thoughts are connected to the self-concept (Greenwald et al., 2002), and the term *insight*, which is associated with "sudden understanding of a problem" (Skaar & Reber, 2020, p. 49). The theme has similarities with an "aha" experience (Bowden, Beeman, Fleck, & Kounios, 2005; Skaar & Reber, 2020), which is described as "a peculiar yet pleasurable experience that occurs after a sudden insight" (Skaar & Reber, 2020, p. 49). Suddenness, positive affect, and a sense of understanding are parts of an "aha" experience (ib.). Creative insight and personal transformation are often associated with supernatural influence, whereby this influence was originally denoted as inspiration (Thrash & Elliot, 2004).

In sum, the theme of personal insight highlights that customer inspiration adds value apart from the transactional relationship, as one expert described it as "consumption plus X". The X stimulates cognitive processes that can result in an "aha" experience.

Table 1.6 Illustrative respondent statements for the "personal insight" dimension

- *"I think the shift is a level of consciousness. There are people in life, [...] consumers, professionals, that are wanting more than just transactional relationships. They want relationships that deeply connect them with some sort of transformation, some sort of growth" (R1).*
- *"We love creativity and want to encourage our customers to design their homes creatively and according to their own wishes and needs" (R2, translated from German).*
- *"While I have just described that in the past, the topic came functionally and emotionally, i.e. functional inspiration and then the emotional inspiration, in my opinion today the topic comes through, which is always explained as "the next big thing" [...], purpose" (R3, translated from German).*
- *"That's why nowadays you should ask yourself to what extent you can inspire consumers with the triple: functional, emotional, meaningful" (R3, translated from German).*
- *"We actually said, look how do you find this dream of the big wide world, (...), so maybe we inspired you to listen to yourself again a bit and do things that you really enjoy" (R5, translated from German).*
- *"If you don't manage to inspire your customers and create added value for your customers, you will be lost in the masses. We want to help them to change their mindset and offer them beautiful alternatives through our concept, such as how they can consume better, what they have to pay attention to when they buy a garment" (R6, translated from German).*
- *"Inspiration very often means to bring people to something they never thought of before" (R7, translated from German).*

1.4.3.3 Deep Connection

Many experts linked inspiration with a "deep emotion" (R1). As one interviewee said: "If I'm going to arouse emotions, I want them to be positive. That means ultimately I do it with the goal of identification. And I think that's (…) inspiration" (R7). Other statements included the notion that inspiration "is coming from a deep connected feeling" (R1) that "opens up a certain emotional world" (R5). We named this third theme as *deep connection*.

The theme addresses the relationship that a customer establishes with an organization or brand though inspiration. Similar to the *connection* characteristic by Hart (1998), *deep connection* describes a shift in boundaries between a customer and brand. The relationship is characterized by a strong connection as one form of a customer-brand relationship (Fournier, 1998). As "customer inspiration is a deep emotion" (R1), it has similarities with the emotional attachment construct (Thomson, MacInnis, & Park, 2005). Further, the connection between a customer and brand is somewhat reminiscent to the construct of brand attachment, which is defined as "the strength of the cognitive and affective bond connecting the brand with the self" (Park & Macinnis, 2006, p. 194). Connection through inspiration extends beyond "loyalty" (R1). Personal insight and deep connection are two key themes for customer inspiration that together enable "identification" (R7) with the brand. Table 1.7 provides an overview of expert statements related to deep connection.

Table 1.7 Illustrative respondent statements for the "deep connection" dimension

- *"For me, it goes far beyond loyalty, Customer inspiration is a deep emotion. [...] When I think about Customer Inspiration I think about it on a very deep level" (R1).*
- *"For me, it is about how we inspire customers to act in a way that it is coming from a deep connected feeling. There is no doubt that Customer inspiration stimulates loyalty but I think inspiration is better than loyalty" (R1).*
- *"[...] which opens up a certain emotional world, which in turn inspires you" (R5, translated from German).*
- *"If I'm going to arouse emotions, I want them to be positive. That means ultimately I do it with the goal of identification. And I think that's [...] inspiration. Triggering something in people" (R7, translated from German).*
- *"The thing I always talk about is really understanding your audience, what they care about. So if you don't know what is really going to make an impact on them, then you can't inspire them. You have to figure out what matters to them, what they care about, what they are thinking about or you have to know what they don't care about and what they are not thinking about, so you get their attention by making them think about a new idea" (R8).*
- *"I think most of how you inspire customers comes from how I know my customers and how I try to understand them" (R11, translated from German).*

1.4.4 Conceptual Framework of Customer Inspiration

Before delineating customer inspiration from other constructs, this chapter summarizes the results from the expert interviews and presents some propositions about its nomological network. These propositions are grounded in the expert interviews as well as existing literature. However, to a certain degree they are unavoidably speculative.

When a customer is inspired, he/she is activated by the brand to follow its mission, suggestion or ideas. The phenomenon includes cognitive, affective, and behavioral elements, which are reflected in its three themes of personal insight, deep connection, and activation. With its cognitive, affective, and behavioral manifestation with no fixed hierarchy, customer inspiration joins the list of integrative marketing models (Vakratsas & Ambler, 1999).

In order to enable identification, experts state that organizations or brands need to be authentic (R5, R6, R10), which is also referred to as "genuine", "real", or "truthful" (Kennick, 1985). Bruhn, Schoenmüller, Schäfer, and Heinrich (2012) identified four dimensions of brand authenticity, namely continuity, originality, reliability, and naturalness. Groves (2001) describes brand authenticity as the uniqueness, culture or tradition of a company. Being real and truthfulness enable the connection between a customer and brand. We propose that the more authentic a brand is perceived by a customer, the closer and deeper the connection between the customer and brand, which in turn results in a higher level of customer inspiration. We propose the following:

P1:   Brand authenticity is an enabler of customer inspiration.

The experts underlined that relevance is a key requirement for customer inspiration (R5, R10, R11). Brand relevance describes the meaningfulness and appropriateness of a brand (Khan, 2009). Perceived personal relevance occurs when an individual's needs, goals, and values can be linked with a product (Celsi & Olson, 1988). It is triggered by either situational sources such as marketing stimuli that are associated with important consequences, goals, and values, or intrinsic sources through "associations between objects and/or actions and important self-relevant consequences, such as the attainment of goals and/or maintenance of values" (Celsi & Olson, 1988, p. 212). Both sources might lead to inspiration as long as they are related to the customer's identity (Sheehan & Dommer, 2020). In order to be receptive to a deep connection with a brand, customers need to feel that they share common goals, motives, and values, which in turn means that brands have to be relevant to customers. Regarding the relevance of a brand, we propose the following:

P2:   Brand relevance is an enabler of customer inspiration.

In our interviews we also asked the experts about what drives customer inspiration. We could identify one driver of inspiration which we call brand purpose. We understand brand purpose as a marketing stimulus that provides additional meaning to customers besides product benefits and image components. This is in line with Fournier (1998) who states that "brand relationship quality evolves through meaningful brand and consumer actions" (p. 365). Hence, proposition 3 is stated as follows:

P3:   Brand purpose is an enabler of customer inspiration.

As maximizing customer inspiration is not the ultimate goal for managers but rather a way to create competitive advantages, it holds particular interest which direct and indirect outcomes can be predicted by customer inspiration. As with the most customer-brand relation constructs (Khamitov et al., 2019), customer inspiration could also drive customer brand loyalty, which appears to be a useful indicator for financial performance (Smith & Wright, 2004). Brand loyalty is defined as the "constancy of a consumer 's brand preference over time" (Khamitov et al., 2019, p. 441). As brand loyalty is a consequence of brand attachment, brand love, brand trust, brand identification, and self-brand connection (Khamitov et al., 2019), we believe that customer inspiration also leads to brand loyalty. Therefore, we propose the following:

P4:   Brand loyalty is a consequence of customer inspiration.

While these four propositions only capture a snapshot of the nomological network of customer inspiration, they provide a useful first idea of what surrounds the construct.

1.4.5 Distinction Between Customer Inspiration and Other Constructs

This chapter aims to conceptually distinguish customer inspiration from other constructs and examine the conceptual relationship with related constructs. At the end of this section, we summarize the main results graphically (Figure 1.1).

Customer Inspiration and Customer Engagement
Similar to customer inspiration, customer engagement is a rather new construct with growing prominence in marketing science. It connects the term "engagement", which has been discussed to date in various disciplines such as sociology, political science, and psychology, as well as the marketing domain (Brodie et al., 2011). The construct describes an interactive customer-brand relationship (Linda Hollebeek, 2011b) that can be defined as "customers' behavioral manifestations that have a brand- or firm-focus, beyond purchase, resulting from motivational drivers" (Marketing Science Institute, 2010, p. 254). Many different definitions of customer (or consumer or customer-brand) engagement exist. Since customer engagement seems to be the most closely related construct to customer inspiration, a detailed examination of customer engagement seems necessary. Appendix 2 within the Electronic Supplementary Material provides an overview of the most commonly-used definitions of engagement in the marketing literature. Although clear similarities exist between the two constructs, significant differences prompt us to assume that the two constructs have distinct properties. First, we highlight the similarities, before moving to the differences. The five fundamental propositions (FP1–FP5) of Brodie et al. (2011)—which are the outcome of a meta-study on existing customer engagement findings—provide the rough structure of this discussion.

Both constructs represent a psychological state (FP1). Apart from a few unidimensional conceptualizations of customer engagement (e.g., Schivinski, Christodoulides, & Dabrowski, 2016), the multidimensional view of customer engagement with behavioral, emotional, and cognitive dimensions prevails (e.g., Brodie et al., 2011; Higgins, 2006; Linda Hollebeek, 2011b; Pansari & Kumar, 2017). Multidimensionality represents a common characteristic of both constructs. Depending on the context setting, the expression of the dimensions may vary (FP4). We assume that this is also true for customer inspiration. For instance, the behavioral dimension could be reflected by imaginary stimulation or interaction with the brand, like sharing brand-related content. The level of intensity of customer engagement as well as customer inspiration may change depending on the experience (FP5).

In accordance with the conceptualization of customer engagement, the two constructs also share common themes. *Connection* is mentioned by Vivek et al. (2012), who define customer engagement as "the intensity of an individual's participation in and connection with an organization's offerings or activities". Offerings are further described as brands, or goods, while activities could be interactive activities on company websites (Vivek et al., 2012). In a later work by Vivek, Beatty, Dalela, and Morgan (2014, p. 401), the authors specify the theme as *social connection*, "often involving others in the social network created around the brand/offering/activity". So, King, and Sparks (2012, p. 310) define customer engagement as "customers' personal connection to a brand as manifested in cognitive, affective, and behavioral actions outside of the purchase situation". Kumar and Pansari (2016, p. 499) describe engagement as "the attitude, behavior and the level of connectedness" between a customer and a firm. The two constructs share the theme of *connection*. In addition, *activation* appears in some conceptualizations of consumer engagement (Linda Hollebeek, 2011b; Linda Hollebeek, Glynn, & Brodie, 2014; Van Doorn et al., 2010). *Activation* represents a customer's energy and time spent interacting with a brand (Linda Hollebeek, 2011b) and it summarizes the actions involving the brand and its products and services offered (Vivek, 2009). *Activation* partly overlaps with FP1 by Brodie et al. (2011, p. 258), which describes customer engagement as "an interactive customer experience with a focal agent/object (…)". The theme of *personal insight* is explicitly part of the consumer engagement conceptualization, although cognitive manifestations occur as cognitive presence (Yu et al., 2015), cognitive activity (Linda Hollebeek, 2011a), co-creative experience (Brodie et al., 2011), and attitude (Kumar & Pansari, 2016). Both constructs are embedded in a nomological network (FP3). Hence, the concept of engagement should not be observed on its own, but rather in the overall context. Put simply, customer engagement and customer inspiration are both psychological states (FP1). Both are embedded in a wider nomological network (FP3) and they are multidimensional concepts with cognitive, emotional, and behavioral dimensions (FP4). Both can occur with different levels (FP5) and they share the themes of *connection* and *activation*.

It will be depicted in the following what makes these two constructs distinct. The most striking difference is that customer engagement is subject to the principles of service-dominant logic (FP1) (Brodie et al., 2011; Linda Hollebeek, 2011a). Within this logic, the customer takes an active, co-creating role with the company by entering into a dialogue (e.g. in the form of feedback; FP2) and creating unique experiences with the object from which the brand can benefit (Prahalad & Ramaswamy, 2004). These two-way interactions between both parties are an obligatory condition of customer engagement, which has its conceptual foundations in interactivity (Gambetti & Graffigna, 2010; Linda Holle-beek, 2011b). When a customer is inspired, he/she also becomes activated, but he/she does not necessarily have to co-create value for the brand by interact-ing with the brand. The interaction is rather one-way, directed from the brand to the individual and triggering something within the recipient. As for customer engagement, inspiration creates something valuable, but rather in the form of a transformational idea or "aha" experience without necessary participation with the brand or within the service relationship setting. In contrast to customer engage-ment—which requires a participation, defined as "the degree to which customers produce and deliver service" (R. Bolton & Saxena-Iyer, 2009; Brodie et al., 2011, p. 261)—customer inspiration does not require any kind of participation. Another difference concerns the outcomes of consumer engagement. Potential consequences of customer engagement include "commitment", "self-brand con-nection", and consumers' "emotional brand attachment" (Brodie et al., 2011, p. 260). The latter two are part of customer inspiration, represented by the *deep connection* theme. The third main difference refers to the *personal insight* theme, which stimulates a customer's thinking and can lead to an "aha" experience. This form of insight is not part of consumer engagement.

This discussion shows that the two constructs have similarities—especially in their nature and structure—but they differ in essential characteristics such as par-ticipation in brand activities, the transformational character as part of the *personal insight* theme, and the type of connection between customers and brands.

Customer Inspiration and Brand Love
Definitions and conceptualizations of brand love are widespread. Some researchers associate the concept of brand love with a strong emotion of the consumer towards a brand (Batra et al., 2012; Carroll & Ahuvia, 2006). Carroll and Ahuvia (2006, p. 81) define brand love as "the degree of passionate emo-tional attachment a satisfied consumer has for a particular trade name", which includes "passion for the brand, attachment to the brand, positive evaluation of the brand, positive emotions in response to the brand, and declarations of love for the brand". The conceptualization by Batra et al. (2012) covers a wider domain including cognitions (self-brand integration), emotions (positive emotional con-nection), and passion-driven behaviors that include but extend beyond brand attachment and self-brand connection. For Rossiter (2002), brand love comprises deep affection and separation distress. These definitions and conceptualizations indicate that the similarities of brand love and customer inspiration concern the *deep connection* theme of customer inspiration. "Love" aspects like separation distress, declarations of love, or passion-driven behavior—which are related to

romantic relationships (Shimp & Madden, 1988)—are not part of an inspirational experience. However, emotional attachment is very similar to the *deep connection* theme. Since emotional and brand attachment are independent constructs, we will discuss this in more detail below.

Customer Inspiration and (Brand) Attachment
Grounded in the work of parent-infant relationships (Bowlby, 1977), emotional attachment has been found between many other objects, like pets (Hirschman, 1994) or celebrities (Alperstein, 1991), as well as brands (Schouten & McAlexander, 1995). The latter—also known as *brand attachment*—describes the bond that connects a consumer's self with a brand, including thoughts, memories, and impressions. It is reflected by two factors, namely brand-self connection and brand prominence (Park et al., 2010). The brand-self connection describes the degree of overlap between the brand and the consumer's self, as well as the inclusion of the brand into the self (Chaplin & John, 2005; Escalas & Bettman, 2003). The brand becomes a representation of one's identity and/or goals (Mittal, 2006) and it has emotional and cognitive dimensions (Park et al., 2010). Brand prominence constitutes the presence of the brand in a customer's mind. If memories and thoughts about the brand are easily accessible, the customer often thinks about it. Thus, brand prominence expresses the salience of the relationship (Park et al., 2010). Based on Thomson et al. (2005), consumers' emotional attachment to brands is reflected by three factors of affection, passion, and connection. A *deep connection* between an individual and a brand is also constituent for customer inspiration. In particular, self-brand connection is an important component of customer inspiration. However, the passion component of emotional attachment proceeds too far into a romantic direction and distinguishes the two constructs. Nonetheless, brand attachment and customer inspiration might be strongly correlated.

Customer Inspiration and Brand Attitude
An attitude reflects the evaluation of an object, person, or behavior of someone without direct contact having necessarily been made (Ajzen & Fishbein, 1977; Thomson et al., 2005). Attitude toward the brand is the "individual's internal evaluation of the brand" (Mitchell & Olson, 1981, p. 318). The major common aspect among the variety of definitions of (brand) attitude is the "evaluative (pro-con, pleasant-unpleasant) nature" (Ajzen, 1988, p. 4). Customer inspiration and brand attitude share similarities. Both constructs are of a psychological nature, referring to a brand and incorporating a kind of assessment. Both are multidimensional constructs comprising cognitive, affective, and behavioral components (Ajzen, 1988). Further, both constructs have an effect on consumer behavior.

Brand attitude leads to brand purchase, repeat purchase, and the willingness to recommend a brand (Park et al., 2010). For customer inspiration, we propose an effect on customer loyalty (see section 1.4.4). However, the two constructs can also be differentiated in several aspects, such as the notion that customer inspiration and brand attitude differ in the type of affect that they imply. Brand attitude—although potentially favorable—reflects a rather "cold" affection (Joel Cohen & Areni, 1991; Park et al., 2010), of which consumers can have any number towards brands or objects with relatively little importance in their lives (Thomson et al., 2005). By contrast, customer inspiration has a rather "warm" character due to the deep connection that the individual creates with a brand. This special connection is rare and precious. In addition, brand attitude reflects an individual's evaluation of a brand that is relatively enduring (Linda Hollebeek, 2011b). Customer inspiration appears rather sudden and in a rush, similar to "aha" experiences (Skaar & Reber, 2020).

Customer Inspiration, Customer Co-Creation, and Customer Orientation
Customer co-creation is part of innovation research and studies about the construct deal with the inflow of knowledge from customers to create better internal innovations (Pee, 2016). Similar to customer engagement, customer co-creation is a concept "that explain[s] joint configuration of value and non-transactional behavior" (Fernandes & Remelhe, 2016, pp. 311, 312). When customers co-create, they want to create "value to build their identities, express themselves creatively, socialize with other consumers and enjoy unique and memorable experiences" (ib.). The construct of customer co-creation is related to customer inspiration. However, some may confuse the two concepts if the latter is misinterpreted. Customer inspiration describes a personal phenomenon that comprises an emotional, cognitive, and behavioral component. It describes the level of identification with a brand's mindset or action and triggers a customer to follow the brand, either ideologically or behaviorally. By contrast, during customer co-creation the role of the customer changes and he/she participates within the creation of marketing value (Fernandes & Remelhe, 2016). It is therefore a special form of engagement.

Similar to customer co-creation, customer orientation is another construct that can be confused with customer inspiration. Customer orientation describes the extent to which a firm "engages in efforts to understand, serve, and satisfy its consumers" (Chakravarty, Kumar, & Grewal, 2014, p. 2). It is also the mechanism behind engaging consumers (Chakravarty et al., 2014). This construct describes a company strategy rather than a consumer-brand relationship.

Delineation of Different Definitions of Customer Inspiration

As mentioned in section 1.2.2, previous work on customer inspiration has been published (Böttger, 2015; Böttger et al., 2017; Rudolph et al., 2012). The study of customer inspiration developed by Böttger et al. (2017, p. 117) defines the construct as "a customer's temporary motivational state that facilitates the transition from the reception of a marketing-induced idea to the intrinsic pursuit of a consumption-related goal". Our definition shares similarities with Böttger et al. (2017), while also differing in essential aspects. For both, the notion applies that customer inspiration is caused by a marketing stimulus. Further, they both describe an event or phenomenon of a rather short timeliness. As a motivational state, Böttger et al. (2017, p. 118) split customer inspiration into an activation and intention component, described as "inspired-by" and "inspired-to". Both components are necessary for a customer inspiration episode. The activation phase includes a "shift in customer awareness toward new possibilities", a "moment of sudden realization and insight", and the fact that "customers may then experience transcendence toward a new state of mind" (Böttger et al., 2017, p. 118). The activation component is quite similar to the *personal insight* dimension of our conceptualization of customer inspiration. However, we more strongly emphasize the transformational aspect compared with Böttger et al. (2017). As part of the intention component, "customers experience an urge to actualize the new idea (e.g., by purchasing and using a product) (…)" (Böttger et al., 2017, p. 119). This component has similarities with our *activation* theme, but the "consumption-related goal" (Böttger et al., 2017, p. 117) links inspiration to a transaction situation. This is different from our understanding of what customer inspiration is, whereby a consumer can be inspired by a brand and does not necessarily have to be a customer (yet), nor in the short-term future. A transaction is desirable from a marketing or business perspective, but the time lag between the inspiration moment and purchase behavior is undefined. The activation can even only comprise engaging with the brand by e.g. sharing content or stimulated imagination of a certain situation. Another aspect is that customer inspiration in this study is not split in two components, but rather it is reflected by three dimensions (themes) with no strict order. Furthermore, our definition of customer inspiration describes the identification with a brand's mindset and actions, which assumes a *deep connection* between both parties. This connection or the emotional component in general is not covered by Böttger et al. (2017). In summary, the two customer inspiration definitions and conceptualizations share common aspects, but the transformational character and the deep connection theme of our definition differentiates us from Böttger et al. (2017).

In this chapter, we have compared customer inspiration with related constructs and discussed similarities and differences, as summarized in Table 1.8.

Table 1.8 Differentiation of constructs related to customer inspiration

Concept	Definition	Conceptual Differentiation from CI	Author(s)
Customer engagement	The intensity of a consumer's participation and connection with an organization's offerings and/or its organized activities	Unlike CI, customer engagement is subject to the principles of service-dominant relationships and pursues participation	Linda Hollebeek (2011a), Kumar and Pansari (2016), Vivek (2009)
Brand love	The degree of passionate emotional attachment that a satisfied consumer has with a particular trade name	Unlike CI, brand love describes a passion-driven ("hot") and romantic relationship	Batra et al. (2012), Carroll and Ahuvia (2006)
Brand attachment	The strength of the bond connecting the brand with the self	Although closely related, brand attachment reflects a strong passion component, unlike CI	Park et al. (2010), Park et al. (2013), Thomson et al. (2005)
Brand attitude	An individual's internal evaluation of the brand	Compared with CI, brand attitude reflects a rather "cold" affect as well as an individual's evaluation of a brand that is relatively enduring	Mitchell and Olson (1981), Rossiter (2014) Thomson et al. (2005)
Customer inspiration by Böttger et al. (2017)	A customer's temporary motivational state that facilitates the transition from the reception of a marketing-induced idea to the intrinsic pursuit of a consumption-related goal	Unlike CI by Böttger et al. (2017), CI based on this study includes an emotional component described as a deep connection between a customer and brand, as well as a clearer transformational character	Böttger et al. (2017)
Customer co-creation	A concept that explains the joint configuration of value and non-transactional behavior	Unlike CI, customer co-creation reflects the changed role of the customer when he/she participates within the creation of marketing value	Fernandes and Remelhe (2016)
Customer orientation	The extent to which a firm engages in efforts to understand, serve, and satisfy its consumers	Unlike CI, customer orientation describes a company strategy	Chakravarty et al. (2014)

Note: CI = Customer Inspiration

In the Venn diagram (Figure 1.1) representation of the essential constructs, it becomes clear that there are three overarching dimensions (themes) that occur within the examined constructs. *Activation* is part of consumer engagement, customer inspiration (Böttger et al., 2017) and customer co-creation, *connection* is part of brand attachment, brand love and customer engagement, while *insight* is part of customer inspiration by Böttger et al. (2017). Our understanding of customer inspiration derived from expert interviews and literature work incorporates all three themes.

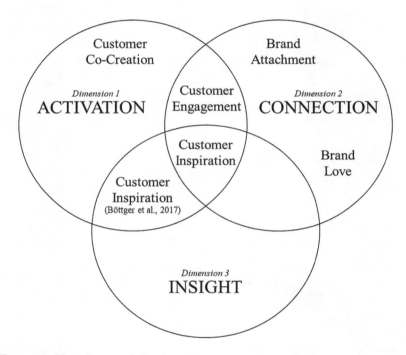

Figure 1.1   Venn diagram of related constructs

1.5   Discussion

Companies with loyal customers financially outperform others (N. A. Morgan & Rego, 2006), have increased WOM (G. Watson et al., 2015), and—regarding attitudinal loyalty—they are less price-sensitive and spend more (Umashankar, Bhagwat, & Kumar, 2017). In order to create customer loyalty, companies need to build a sustainable customer-brand relationship and attach consumers (Khamitov et al., 2019; Mende, Bolton, & Bitner, 2013), drive brand love (Batra et al., 2012), and customer engagement (Gavilanes, Flatten, & Brettel, 2018) or—as proposed in this study—inspire customers. Existing literature about the customer inspiration construct is still thin in the marketing field. We believe that customer inspiration is a promising and important construct to establish long-term relationships with customers. With our study, we advance the knowledge about this phenomenon though defining and conceptualizing it. Based on twelve expert interviews, we extracted and built marketing theory through the theories-in-use approach (Zeithaml et al., 2020). In the following, our findings are discussed along the research questions.

RQ1:   How should customer inspiration be defined?

A literature review of inspiration in general and the marketing field delivered a thorough overview of existing definitions and descriptions of the phenomenon. In marketing, the topic is quite new, and only few definitions of customer inspiration exist to date. We derived our definition based on a detailed analysis of expert knowledge and a post-hoc literature review. We define customer inspiration as the level of an individual's identification with and activation through a brand's mindset and actions. The individuals can be current or potential consumers.

RQ2:   How can customer inspiration be conceptualized?

Customer inspiration is manifested cognitively, affectively, and behaviorally. The cognitive and affective elements of customer inspiration incorporate e.g. "aha" experiences, feelings, and insights of customers, while the behavioral elements capture the activation of customers, both within and outside of the direct consumer-brand encounter. Customer inspiration involves a deep connection that individuals form with brands, based on their personal experiences with the mindset and actions of the brand. Inspired customers build authenticity-based relationships through intense identification with the brand.

We identified three themes that are part of every customer inspiration experience. Inspiration includes a moment of *activation*, which can take the form of a real action or cognition. Studies about inspiration in the field of psychology have also identified *energy* and *motivation* as equivalent characteristics (Hart, 1998; Thrash & Elliot, 2003). As the second theme, *personal insight* reflects the cognitive component of customer inspiration, similarly to the *opened* and *clarity* characteristic of Hart (1998) or the *transcendence* component of Thrash and Elliot (2003). It includes new thoughts or ideas that have a transformative character and are connected to the self-concept. *Personal insight* has similarities with an "aha" experience (Bowden et al., 2005; Skaar & Reber, 2020) in terms of suddenness, and understanding. The third theme of *deep connection* reflects the emotional dimension in the form of a bond between a customer's self and a brand. This connection and transformative moment leads to an identification with the brand. *Connection* has been also identified as one of the four key characteristics of inspiration (Hart, 1998). Overall, we understand customer inspiration as a form of customer-brand relationship (Khamitov et al., 2019). As the concept is based on human-like relationships that consumers form with brands (Fournier, 1998), customer inspiration is the equivalent to the relationship between a charismatic leader in an organizational setup and his/her followers. The underlying force of a charismatic relationship is a strong connection between the followers' self-concept and the leader (Howell & Shamir, 2005), whereby inspiring brands manage to create a connection with consumers and their self-concept.

We further identified three enablers of customer inspiration, namely brand authenticity, brand relevance and brand purpose. Authentic brands are perceived as real, original and natural (Bruhn et al., 2012; Groves, 2001). We propose that an unpretentious brand image that relies on naturalness is the route to consumers' souls as it enables identification and consequently inspiration. An example of naturalness comes from the music industry: in 2014, the music artist Beyoncé launched a music video that—unlike conventional music videos—was produced in an unedited and amateur-like style (Beyoncé, 2014). In her highly successful clip, she provided a glimpse into her private life and appeared like a woman "just like us", which is far away from the typically unachievable far-away style of popstars and thus enabled identification with her (Nicholson, 2014). The second enabler of customer inspiration that we propose is brand relevance, which describes how meaningful and appropriate a brand is to consumers (Khan, 2009). A recent example of how brands are trying to be relevant is Edeka, the supermarket company, which launched a TV spot during Christmas season 2020 covering current topics. The spot tells a story about the dark side of the COVID-19 pandemic and the upside effects of neighborhood support (Campillo-Lundbeck,

2020). The actual supermarket products are not in the focus of the clip. The story is emotionally touching, addresses the issue of intercultural friendship and activates thinking about vulnerable groups around us. Our third proposed enabler of customer inspiration is brand purpose, which describes *why* brands exist (Sinek, 2011). Brands that show attitude as well as purpose and incorporate this into their marketing communication have increasingly appeared in recent years (Levine, 2019).

RQ3:   *What is the difference between customer inspiration and other related constructs?*

We analyzed established constructs like customer engagement (Brodie et al., 2011; Vivek et al., 2012), brand love (Batra et al., 2012), and brand attachment (Park et al., 2010). Among these constructs, we found similarities and differences compared with customer inspiration defined by us. Interestingly, all of them are somewhat connected. Customer engagement shares an activation and connection dimension with customer inspiration, while emotional attachment components of brand love and brand attachment are similar to the *deep connection* theme of customer inspiration. In the definition by Böttger et al. (2017), we identified an activation and insight component. Our conceptualization of customer inspiration connects all three components. A key differentiator is the transformational character of a moment of inspiration. As experts described it as "change in mindset", customers' inspiration can trigger thoughts that have a transformative character or enable a "sudden understanding of a problem" (Skaar & Reber, 2020, p. 49). Similar to an "aha" experience (Bowden et al., 2005), inspiring brands enable consumers' thoughts to thrive.

Directions for Further Research
This study certainly has some limitations. First, the differentiation between customer inspiration and related constructs was only conducted conceptually. Empirical evidence of whether the corresponding constructs are distinct from each other remains outstanding. A study that demonstrates the convergent and discriminant validity of customer inspiration and constructs like brand attachment and brand attitude would help to underline the conceptual distinction and importance of the construct. We will try to fill this gap in **Study III** where we compare customer inspiration with the established brand attitude construct.

Second, although we provide a detailed conceptualization of customer inspiration, verification of whether the construct adds practical value has not been provided with this study. Further examination is necessary concerning whether customer inspiration has the explanatory and predicative power to compete with established mediator variables like brand attitude or brand attachment. Brand attitude has been identified as a key antecedent of consumer behavior (Park et al., 2010). Many studies are dedicated towards attitude formation and its predictive relevance (Lutz, 1975; Udell, 1965). Whether the measurement of customer inspiration adds value to marketing managers in terms of its different behavioral implications compared with other established constructs needs to be investigated in future studies. We will address this in our **Study III** where we compare the explanatory power of customer inspiration and brand attitude.

Third, our new definition of customer inspiration needs a measurement tool to assess and manage the construct. Existing measuring tools of inspiration by Thrash and Elliot (2003) or Böttger et al. (2017) do not match the conceptualization of the focal construct of our study. A new operationalization is necessary and needs to be developed and validated in further studies accordingly. We will elaborate on this topic in **Study II**.

Fourth, the question of what drives customer inspiration has not been answered with our study. Although we propose that a brand's authenticity, relevance and purpose enable customers to become inspired, an empirical examination of key antecedents is necessary. First source characteristics of customer inspiration like product bundles or product-in-use presentations have been proposed by Böttger et al. (2017) and Rudolph and Pfrang (2014). Ikea—the furniture retail company—was named as an example of a company that manages customer inspiration well (Rudolph et al., 2012). However, some of our experts stated that Ikea is merely a master at creating brand awareness and presenting their products, but a not really inspiring brand. We support this idea as it is in line with our understanding of customer inspiration. Therefore, future studies should focus on identifying drivers that can be implemented by practitioners.

Study II: Measurement Model of Customer Inspiration

Abstract

Investing in customers' inspiration seems to be a promising marketing strategy to build brand equity and increase sales performance. Grounded in psychology, the state of inspiration has recently also attracted the attention of marketing researchers as a driver of attitudinal, emotional, and behavioral consequences. Current work on the construct's definition and conceptualization exhibits some shortcomings. We therefore redefined customer inspiration, based on expert interviews, as the level of identification with and activation through a brand's mindset and action. Further, we conceptualized the construct as multidimensional with three main themes, namely activation, personal insight and deep connection. Building upon this, the study operationalized customer inspiration within a six-step index development procedure. We developed a measurement model based on literature, focus groups, a qualitative survey, and validation interviews to ensure content validity of the construct and validated it by means of two empirical studies. As a result, we specify customer inspiration as a formative second-order construct with three reflective first-order components, connection, transformation and activation, which can be assessed with our nine-item measure.

A previous conceptual version of this article was submitted as a project study for the Master of Business Research (Ludwig-Maximilians-Universität, Munich) in December 2019.

Supplementary Information The online version contains supplementary material available at (https://doi.org/10.1007/978-3-658-35894-5_2).

2.1   Motivation

Marketing managers are confronted with two significant challenges at present. Firstly, due to the complex world that is characterized by volatility, uncertainty, complexity, and ambiguity (VUCA), well-established marketing strategies must be reassessed (Brooks, 2016). Geopolitical challenges, climate change, and evolving social values create an atmosphere of uncertainty for consumers (Kantar, 2019). Secondly, in saturated markets, companies have to differentiate from competitors and create distinguishing features in order to find access to consumers (Meffert, Bruhn, & Hadwich, 2018). Otherwise, companies' offerings will dissolve in the overwhelming information and advertising overload that consumers face (Ansari & Mela, 2003). According to a study by Kantar (2019), *meaningful* brands are the ones that are able to stand out from competition and gain value during these challenging times. Brands are meaningful for consumers when they are able to create "a broad and deep set of mental associations" which, among others, refer to consumers' innate needs (Kantar, 2019, p. 6). In marketing science, the meaningfulness of a brand often correlates with the relevance of a brand (Khan, 2009). Perceived personal relevance occurs when an individual's needs, goals, and values are linked with a product (Celsi & Olson, 1988). Each year, the marketing agency Prophet (2019) tries to analyze what it takes to make a brand relevant by means of the Prophet Brand Relevance Index® and asks 50,000 consumers which brands are most relevant to them and why. In their 2019 report they state: "The most relevant brands are centered on a clear, authentic purpose. They enable connectivity, but go beyond that to create true connection and a sense of community" (Prophet, 2019, p. 4). The agency identified four common principles which make brands relevant to their consumers. Besides being innovative, making consumers' lives easier, and designing products and services that "meet important needs in peoples' lives", brands also need to inspire (Prophet, 2019, p. 7).

The fact that meaningful brands inspire consumers is in line with our propositions from **Study I**. In this study, we examined current definitions of inspiration in psychology and marketing and concluded that customer inspiration is a promising factor for marketing communication and brand building strategies. However, further definitional and conceptual work was necessary to capture the construct. According to the theories-in-use approach (Zeithaml et al., 2020), we conducted expert interviews to extract theory about customer inspiration from the "real world". As a result, we defined customer inspiration as the level of an individual's identification with, and activation through, a brand's mindset and actions. We further conceptualized customer inspiration as a multidimensional construct with three main themes: activation, deep connection, and personal insight. This definition and conceptualization shares common aspects with existing work by Böttger et al. (2017), but it differentiates itself with regard to its transformational character and the deep connection that customers build with brands when they feel inspired.

Relationships between customers and brands enjoy growing importance in the scientific community (Fetscherin & Heinrich, 2015; Khamitov et al., 2019). Several constructs "reflect the types of ties that develop between consumers and brands" (Khamitov et al., 2019, pp. 435–436), like brand attachment (Park et al., 2010), brand love (Batra et al., 2012), self-brand connection (Escalas & Bettman, 2003), and brand identification (Stokburger-Sauer et al., 2012). Customer inspiration might be another factor among these customer-brand relationship constructs that is a positive predictor of brand loyalty (Homburg, Wieseke, & Hoyer, 2009; Khamitov et al., 2019). In this case, the relationship between customers and brands has a transformative character, similar to the bond between charismatic leaders and their followers (Conger & Kanungo, 1987).

Many firms use the term *inspiration* in their marketing activities. One example is GoPro that states: "GoPro frees people to celebrate the moment, inspiring others to do the same" (GoPro, 2020). The brand dominates the market of action cameras worldwide, and had a market share of 87% in 2018 in the US camcorder market (Handelsblatt, 2019). The brand is known for cameras and accessories that can capture experiences which can be shared with others. With their claims "GoPro—Be a hero" and "GoPro—Ignite your creativity", the brand sells the idea of breaking free, celebrating the moment, and inspiring others (GoPro, 2019).

For the creation of inspiring brands and advertisements, an assessment tool is needed to measure the level of customer inspiration evoked. Literature already provides a few measures to assess (customer) inspiration, e.g., the customer inspiration scale by Böttger et al. (2017) and the inspiration scale by Thrash and Elliot (2003). However, these measurement models are based on a different conceptualization of the construct. We need a new measurement model that meets the requirements and content specifications of our understanding of customer inspiration. This study aims to develop such a measurement model. We see two important aspects that should be taken into account for this endeavor. Firstly, the model needs to be designed as a relevant and rigorous tool to enable managers and scientists to assess customer inspiration with all its facets and in an economical way. Secondly, it needs to be correctly specified to prevent measurement errors (Jarvis et al., 2003).

This study undertakes several approaches of a qualitative and quantitative nature to meet these requirements. The overarching goal of this study was to operationalize the construct and create a reliable and valid measuring model of customer inspiration. For this purpose, we followed the C-OAR-SE procedure (Rossiter, 2002) and took recommendations by Diamantopoulos and Winklhofer (2001) into account. Our index development procedure includes six steps to accomplish this goal. In the first part, we develop a measurement model in four steps including a literature review, focus group sessions, a qualitative study, and validation interviews. In the second part, the measurement model is validated by means of two empirical studies to streamline the item battery, create the final index, and to assess its external validity.

This study is structured as follows: First, we give an overall overview about inspiration and existing measurement methods of (customer) inspiration in particular. In doing this, we not only focus on scientific publications, but also on measurement scales used by practitioners. Second, we examine the findings and conceptualization of customer inspiration as well as its dimensions that are based on the managerial perspective. This leads to the development of the measurement model. Implications for theory and practice will conclude this study.

2.2   Theoretical Background

In this chapter we provide an overview of the different ways to assess (customer) inspiration. At present, only a few measurement models of customer inspiration exist. A potential reason for this could be that essential work for inspiration in the field of marketing research has been published in recent years (Böttger et al., 2017; Rudolph et al., 2012; Rudolph & Pfrang, 2014). This work also included the development and validation of a customer inspiration scale (Böttger et al., 2017). Studies that deal with customer inspiration have used this measurement model to assess the construct (e.g. Rauschnabel et al., 2019). Measuring customer inspiration is not an easy task, as inspiration is a subtle and abstract phenomenon (see **Study I**), which defies an exact measurement. The existing measurement models of customer inspiration are discussed alongside relevant findings of the overall construct in the following section. Apart from the marketing domain, inspiration in the field of psychology will be considered as well, in order to provide the most comprehensive overview possible.

Customer Inspiration in the Field of Marketing
The most elaborate measurement model of customer inspiration is the customer inspiration scale by Böttger et al. (2017). The authors define customer inspiration as "a customer's temporary motivational state that facilitates the transition from the reception of a marketing-induced idea to the intrinsic pursuit of a

consumption-related goal" (Böttger et al., 2017, p. 117). They conceptualize the construct as a two-factor model that is reflected by the two components, *inspired-by* and *inspired-to*. Each component is measured reflectively by means of 5 indicators. The exact items are shown in Appendix 1 within the Electronic Supplementary Material. The *inspired-by* items assess the more cognitive aspects of customer inspiration that describe a customer's expanded perspective and the discovery of new ideas. The *inspired-to* items reflect the impulse towards internal and external reactions in connection with purchase situations (Böttger et al., 2017).

Certain consequences for inspired customers have been identified. The three main emotional consequences are positive affect (Böttger, 2015; D. Watson, Clark, & Tellegen, 1988), transcendent customer experience (Böttger et al., 2017; Schouten, McAlexander, & Koenig, 2007), and customer delight (Böttger et al., 2017; Oliver & Rust, 1997). In the long run, inspiration can also lead to attitudinal consequences, which reflect evaluations about a company that are more durable than emotions (Böttger et al., 2017). This includes customer satisfaction (Oliver, 1999) and customer loyalty (Verhoef, 2003). As a behavioral consequence, Böttger et al. (2017) investigated the impact of customer inspiration on impulse buying, which is defined as "a consumer's tendency to buy spontaneously, unreflectively, immediately, and kinetically" (Rook & Fisher, 1995, p. 306). Customers who experience an unexpected inspirational influence show a higher intention of unplanned purchases (Böttger et al., 2017). The authors claim that this is particularly true for customers who are prone to spontaneous buying ideas (Rook & Fisher, 1995). Customers with a hedonistic attitude show a higher susceptibility to seeking new experiences. Due to their exploratory behavior, they are more likely to change their purchase plans (Breugelmans & Campo, 2011). Other studies by Böttger et al. (2017) reveal that customer inspiration predicts the number of clicks, products viewed, shopping duration, purchase intentions, and even purchase likelihood (Böttger et al., 2017).

Rauschnabel et al. (2019) applied the customer inspiration scale by Böttger et al. (2017) and examined the influence of inspiration on brand attitude. Within the context of augmented reality, they investigated the effect of customer inspiration on changes in overall brand attitude and showed that inspiration significantly influences the latter (Rauschnabel et al., 2019). Izogo, Mpinganjira, and Ogba (2020) analyzed the effect of customer inspiration on customer citizenship behavior, which is defined as "voluntary and discretionary behaviors that are not required for the successful production and/or delivery of the service but that, in the aggregate, help the service organization overall" (Groth, 2005, p. 11). They show that both components of customer inspiration, *inspired-by* and *inspired-to*, positively affect customer citizenship behaviors. These include an increased number of recommendations, feedback, and sharing of experiences (Izogo et al., 2020). Another study from the tourism industry by Kwon and Boger (2020) examined the connection between brand experience, customer inspiration and pro-environmental intention. The results showed that customer inspiration has a significant effect on pro-environmental intention and at the same time mediates the relationship between brand experience and pro-environmental intention.

Winterich, Nenkov, and Gonzales (2019) also refer to the work of Böttger et al. (2017), but in their study on the role of product transformation salience in the context of recycling, they operationalized customer inspiration slightly differently, with three items that only in part overlap with the customer inspiration scale (see Appendix 1 within the Electronic Supplementary Material for items). The authors provide evidence that due to the customers' inspiration state, transformation salience increases people's intention to recycle (Winterich et al., 2019).

Inspiration in the Field of Psychology
For inspiration in the field of psychology, Thrash and Elliot (2003, 2004) play a significant role as they developed the most commonly used measurement model for inspiration, namely the inspiration scale (e.g. Stephan et al., 2015; Thrash et al., 2017). Thrash and Elliot (2003, p. 872) define "inspiration from above as a motivational state evoked by a revelation (trigger) and directed toward the conversion of transcendent, revealed knowledge into a work of art, a text, or some other concrete form (target)". Within several studies, they built three supplementary frameworks that form the cornerstone for subsequent research about inspiration in the field of psychology (e.g. Stephan et al., 2015; Thrash et al., 2017). Thrash and Elliot (2003, p. 885) conceptualized inspiration as a tripartite construct with "evocation, motivation, and transcendence". They state that inspiration occurs spontaneously, is unplanned, and arises from an unintended situation (evocation). This underlines the fact that inspiration is neither forced nor pressured (Thrash, Elliot, et al., 2010). Inspiration entails motivation because it involves the "energization and direction of behavior" (Thrash & Elliot, 2003, p. 871). Transcendence represents the supernatural essence of inspiration, also described as positivity, enhancement, or clarity (Thrash & Elliot, 2003; Thrash, Elliot, et al., 2010). Additionally, they conceptualized inspiration as having two components, namely *inspired-by* and *inspired-to*. The *inspired-by* component considers the intrinsic appreciation of the pure inspiration stimuli that afterwards is shifted to a motivational state represented by the *inspired-to* component (Thrash & Elliot, 2003, 2004). The third framework explicates inspiration as a transmission model that transforms an antecedent or source (e.g. a creative idea) into an outcome

(e.g. a creative product). Consequently, inspiration functions as a mediator that facilitates this transformation (Thrash, Maruskin, et al., 2010).

The inspiration scale consists of four reflective indicators that imply appraisable statements about inspiration. The scale was first developed to measure the *trait* inspiration (Thrash & Elliot, 2003) and was then adapted to measure the *state* inspiration (Thrash & Elliot, 2004). Whether a scale measures a trait or a state is highly relevant for measurement purposes and has been extensively discussed in psychology research (Allen & Potkay, 1981; Zuckerman, 1983). Whereas traits are "consistent and stable modes of an individual's adjustment to his environment", states reflect a "present activity, temporary states of mind and mood" (Allport & Odbert, 1936, p. 26). For the purpose of this study, only the state of inspiration is of interest. Since the inspiration scale (Thrash & Elliot, 2004) contains the expression *inspiration* in all items, this may pose a validity problem in cases where respondents have different understandings of what inspiration means and therefore interpret the question differently. This can lead to measurement errors (Neuberger, 1974). As definitions and periphrases of inspiration differ widely among scientists, the perceptions among study participants are certainly even more varied since they represent a non-professional audience. However, most of the studies about inspiration use the scale of Thrash and Elliot (2004), with only a few notable exceptions using other approaches (Lockwood, Jordan, & Kunda, 2002). In the latter study, motivation is used as a synonym for inspiration which is assessed by 14 planned effort items.

In social psychology, inspiration is often studied in connection with motivation and creativity. Motivation is about *what* people want and *how* much they want it (Krupić, Banai, & Corr, 2018). Divided into two types, intrinsic motivation refers to the initial free will to act and extrinsic motivation refers to the behavior that is based on the result rather than the activity itself (Ryan & Deci, 2000). The former is positively and the latter is negatively correlated to inspiration (Thrash & Elliot, 2003). Hence, inspiration can affect an individual's values or goals by establishing new standards for evaluating action alternatives (Thrash & Elliot, 2003).

When it comes to creativity, two main views on the relationship between inspiration and creativity exist. Whereas one side views both as synonyms, the other side clearly differentiates between the "appraisal of novelty and usefulness" of creativity and the "motivational state" of inspiration (Oleynick et al., 2014, p. 5). In the study by Thrash and Elliot (2003), inspiration serves as a predictor for indicators of creative output such as patents. They found that patent holders experience inspiration more often than the control group. Furthermore, inspiration also predicts higher ratings of creativity when writing poetry, fiction, or essays (Thrash, Maruskin, et al., 2010). Thrash, Elliot, et al. (2010) also examined the relationship between inspiration and well-being, and found evidence that inspiration enhances well-being as well as positive affect. Subjective well-being is the individual overall life satisfaction evaluation combined with emotional experiences (Diener et al., 2016). Life satisfaction can be influenced, among others, by the intensity of inspiration which functions as a trigger (Thrash, Elliot, et al., 2010).

Tellis et al. (2019) investigated which factors favor virality (i.e. online sharing). Besides drama elements and advert content, various positive emotions were examined, including amusement, excitement, warmth, and inspiration. The studies showed that advertisements which evoke these positive emotions (including inspiration) receive more online shares. If the video contains any drama elements or features celebrities, it intensifies the inspiration effect.

Inspiration in Practice

Whether and how practitioners measure customer inspiration is difficult to assess due to the lack of disclosure. One of the agencies that measure customer inspiration is the marketing agency Prophet, that publishes a brand equity study about the most relevant and influential brands in the US, Germany, UK, and China every year. As a measurement model, they use their Prophet Brand Relevance Index® to evaluate brands. This index contains four dimensions, one of which is the dimension "distinctively inspired" (Prophet, 2019, p. 9). This dimension is measured with four items including "makes me feel inspired", "has a set of beliefs and values that align with my own", "I trust", and "Is modern and in-touch". For Prophet, inspiring brands create a connection with consumers on the emotional level, gain the trust of their customers, and frequently serve a higher purpose. The other three dimensions are "customer obsessed", "ruthlessly pragmatic", and "pervasively innovative". In Germany, for example, the most relevant brand is Apple followed by Lego and Samsung (Prophet, 2019).

The term "inspiration" is often used in advertising. Appendix 2 within the Electronic Supplementary Material shows an exemplary selection of marketing material from various industries. These cases do not necessarily have something to do with the construct customer inspiration as described in this study. In some cases, the expression is used as a synonym for "awareness" or "ideas". Ikea, for instance, gives inspiration/ideas about how a living room could be designed and decorated. The cosmetics brand Maybelline provides tutorials on how to apply makeup, and Siemens Inspirations state that "you will find exciting items for all areas of life that inspire and are fun" (Siemens Home, 2020).

Summary

This literature review shows that existing measurement models of customer inspiration are still rare and are mainly influenced by the conceptualization of customer inspiration by Böttger et al. (2017). The psychology literature provides a more in-depth examination of the trait and state of inspiration as such, and delivers elaborate frameworks of the psychological phenomenon which are also referred to by marketing researchers. The more practice-oriented agency, Prophet, measures inspiration of consumers as one dimension of their Prophet Brand Relevance Index®. The term "inspiration" is quite popular in marketing communication across various industries. How (customer) inspiration is measured is not unanimous, and varies depending on the field of research. All of the measurement scales include the expression *inspire,* which might be misinterpreted by respondents. Customer inspiration by Böttger et al. (2017) as a motivational state consists of an activational and an intentional component, i.e. it consists of an emotional and a cognitive dimension (Ryan & Deci, 2000; Sheeran, 2002). The same applies for inspiration as defined by Thrash and Elliot (2004). Since customer inspiration as defined in **Study I** is conceptually distinct from the models above, an appropriate measurement model needs to be developed. This development process will be discussed and outlined in the following chapters.

2.3 Conceptualization and Index Development Procedure

2.3.1 Definition of Customer Inspiration

The starting point for the index development is the definition of customer inspiration developed in **Study I**. The study at hand aimed to operationalize the construct and to develop a measurement model. Customer inspiration is defined as the level of an individual's identification with, and activation through, a brand's mindset and actions. This definition is based on theoretical results from expert interviews following the theories-in-use approach by Zeithaml et al. (2020). The individuals can be current or potential consumers. **Study I** conceptualized the customer inspiration construct as multidimensional with cognitive, affective, and behavioral elements. The cognitive and affective elements of customer inspiration incorporate the e.g. "aha" experiences, other metacognitive feelings, as well as the transformative thoughts of customers. The behavioral element captures the activation of individuals, both within and outside of the direct consumer-brand encounter. Customer inspiration further involves a strong emotional bond between the individual and a brand, also described as a deep connection, that individuals form with brands based on personal experiences. In the following, the three main themes of customer inspiration namely, personal insight, activation, and deep connection, are described in greater detail. The theme description is based on the findings of **Study I** and extended with additional theoretical background.

Personal Insight

Personal insight is the first theme that characterizes the moment when customers experience inspiration. It is described by three attributes: open mindset, "aha" experience and transformative thoughts, which can occur either in parts or altogether depending on the context.

Open Mindset and Fluency. When a customer is inspired, a general *willingness to new thoughts* or *open mindset* emerges. It reflects the *opened* characteristic of inspiration experiences by Hart (1998) or the transcendence characteristic by Thrash and Elliot (2004). The customer is in a state where he/she is open to new ideas and impressions. This shift in mindset might be an enabler for processing fluency as the "feeling state that helps integrate the experiential components of insight" (Topolinski & Reber, 2010, p. 403). The subjective experience of fluency describes the level of ease or difficulty of cognitive processing (Reber & Greifeneder, 2017). This process occurs when an individual encounters an inspiring brand or advertisement. Processing fluency is also part of an "aha" experience (Skaar & Reber, 2020; Topolinski & Reber, 2010).

"Aha" Experiences. An "aha" experience is an insight, defined as the sudden transition from a state of ignorance to a state of understanding, that "(1) appears suddenly and comes (2) easily in mind, as well as elicits (3) positive affect and (4) subjective certainty in a newfound understanding" (Skaar & Reber, 2020, p. 49). "Aha" experiences increase metacognitive feelings, such as fluency, positive affect, and subjective certainty (Skaar & Reber, 2020). Metacognition covers "subjective experiences or feelings that arise when a mental operation is performed (…)" (Reber & Greifeneder, 2017, p. 3). Also described as "cognition of cognition", metacognition has its roots in education research (Efklides, 2006, p. 3). Metacognitive feelings include "feelings of knowing, feelings of familiarity, feelings of rightness, or feelings of coherence, that all depend on processing fluency" (Reber & Greifeneder, 2017, p. 3). Hence, "aha" experiences are feelings based on mental progress and could also be described as metacognitive or epistemic feelings with cognitive and affective components (Arango-Muñoz, 2014; Arango-Muñoz & Michaelian, 2014; Efklides, 2006).

Transformative Thoughts. The third aspect describes the type of insight. Transformation in the context of advertising has been studied by Puto and Wells (1984), however their view of the expression is slightly different. They characterize transformational advertising as a "warmer, more exciting and/or more enjoyable" experience than "solely from an objective description of the advertised brand"

(Puto & Wells, 1984, p. 638). Further, they describe it as an inseparable connection between the product and the advertisement, so that the customer has to think about the advertisement as soon as he/she uses the product. They refer the notion of "transformational" to the product-advertising relationship, and not to the consumer-brand relation which is more closely related to the case of customer inspiration. Transformational thoughts in the context of customer inspiration are more similar to the transformation enabled by charismatic leaders (Conger & Kanungo, 1987). In this case, the brand acts as a charismatic leader that transforms the "needs, values, preferences and aspirations" of followers, which in such a scenario, are the customers (Shamir et al., 1993, p. 577). Followers are inspired by the brand and its actions as a source of guidance (Yukl, 1998). Charismatic leadership enables a strong connection between the followers' self-concepts and the leader or the collective mission, where followers can identify with either the leader or the collective mission and see the relationship as an opportunity to express aspects of their self-concepts (Howell & Shamir, 2005). As consumers can form human-like relationships to brands (Fournier, 1998), a similar relationship could occur between a charismatic brand and an inspired customer. In this case, a brand shares its mission and gives direction for the individual's actions. The *personal* aspect of the theme personal insight refers to the fact that the insight has a personal touch and that the transformational thoughts are connected to self-concept (Greenwald et al., 2002).

Activation

Activation as one of the basic variables for human behavior is responsible for psychological and motor activity of a human being (Kroeber-Riel, 1979). Inspiration is characterized by a *shift in energy level* (Hart, 1998) that describes the motivational nature of inspiration (Thrash & Elliot, 2003). In the case of customer inspiration, activation can take the form of either real behavior (e.g. sharing the brand with peers or reading more about the brand) or an internal process (e.g. thinking about a certain situation or being motivated to do something). These real behaviors include extra-role behavior of customers like word-of-mouth or recruiting other customers (Ahearne et al., 2005). Activation as a theme of customer inspiration can occur outside the consumer-brand encounter as well and is not limited to the interaction within a service relationship (Patterson & Yu, 2006). When activation occurs as an internal processes, it includes behavioral intentions (Ajzen, 1985) and motivation (Ryan & Deci, 2000), or cognitive imaginations (e.g. abstract self-imagery or imagining using the product) (Hung & Wyer, 2011; Yuwei, Adaval, Steinhart, & Wyer Jr, 2014). The activation is triggered by a marketing stimulus (e.g. an advertising message that transports a certain attitude of a brand or a social activity supported by a brand). Role models inspire people by portraying an idealized version of the self and by demonstrating potential achievements as well as the way of achieving them (Lockwood et al., 2002). Brands trigger similar processes when they inspire customers. To the best of our knowledge, it has not yet been investigated whether brands can also have this "role model" effect on customers, therefore we only propose this similarity.

Deep Connection

We understand customer inspiration as a customer-brand relationship construct (Fournier, 1998) which is characterized by a strong bond between customers and brands reflected in the third theme *deep connection*. This bond is similar to a high level of brand attachment defined as "the cognitive and affective bond connecting the brand with the self" (Park & Macinnis, 2006, p. 194) and results in an identification with the brand (Ahearne et al., 2005).

Brand Attachment. Brand attachment has two components, namely brand-self connection and brand prominence (Park et al., 2010). *Brand-self connection* describes the degree of overlap between the brand and the consumer's self, as well as the inclusion of the brand into the self (Chaplin & John, 2005; Escalas & Bettman, 2003). The brand becomes a representation of one's identity and/or goals (Mittal, 2006) and this phenomenon has emotional and cognitive dimensions (Park et al., 2010). In the case of customer inspiration, the connection between both is specified as "deep" in order to indicate the strength of the connection between consumer and brand. This rather rare connection is enabled by common values and attitudes shared by both parties, similar to a friendship (R. Morgan & Hunt, 1994; van Zalk, Nestler, Geukes, Hutteman, & Back, 2020).

Identification and the Social Identity. Identification is grounded in social psychology and is defined "as the degree to which organizational members perceive themselves and the focal organization as sharing the same defining attributes" (Ahearne et al., 2005, p. 574). One's need for social identity and self-definition is satisfied by identification (Ahearne et al., 2005; Tajfel & Turner, 2004). Customer-company identification, as the "deep, committed, and meaningful relationship(s) that marketers are increasingly seeking to build with their customers" (Bhattacharya & Sen, 2003, p. 76), translates this identification from the employer-employee setting to the consumer-brand environment (Ahearne et al., 2005). Customer inspiration shares the aspects of a deep, committed, and meaningful relationship.

In summary, customer inspiration consists of three themes, namely personal insight, activation, and deep connection. These themes have been derived from expert interviews as well as a post-hoc literature review, and provide crucial content specification for the construct for which a measurement model is developed (Diamantopoulos & Winklhofer, 2001). However, the specification is based only on the managerial perspective. For the development of the measurement model, the consumer perspective is needed in order to develop a rigorous measurement model. A qualitative study has been conducted to cover the consumer's perspective. Details of the overall model construction procedure will be shown in the next subsection.

2.3.2 Index Development Procedure

As customer inspiration is a latent variable, it cannot be directly observed and needs to be operationalized in order to measure it (M. Sarstedt, Ringle, & Hair, 2017). In the previous subsection, the conceptualization of customer inspiration was presented. Its definition and its three themes build the starting point for the scale development. As this conceptualization is based on expert interviews, it mainly reflects the managerial perspective. In order to derive a valid measurement model, the consumer perspective needs to be captured as well. We conducted focus group interviews to address this. For the scale development, we followed the C-OAR-SE procedure introduced by Rossiter (2002) and took suggestions by Diamantopoulos and Winklhofer (2001) and Diamantopoulos (2005) into account to support the index construction by means of statistical analysis. Since we propose a formative measurement model, we developed an index rather than a scale (Rossiter, 2002). In our view, scale development is the umbrella term for scales and indices, and we thus use the expressions synonymously.

Following the nomenclature of the C-OAR-SE procedure, we can define the following preliminary elements: We classify our object as *abstract formed*. An abstract formed object consists of components that "make up the object's meaning" (Rossiter, 2002, p. 310). It applies for customer inspiration as each moment of inspiration contains elements of deep connection, personal insight, and activation. Those together identify an experience of customer inspiration for an individual. The attributes, which describe the dimension against which the customer inspiration is being evaluated, are classified as *eliciting*. Eliciting attributes reflect individual states or dispositions that also apply to customer inspiration. Items are "indicative manifestations" of this state (Rossiter, 2002, p. 316). The raters' entities are identified as *individual* (Rossiter, 2002). We further propose that customer inspiration is a first-order reflective, second-order formed measurement model (Hair, Hult, Ringle, & Sarstedt, 2014; Jarvis et al., 2003; Rossiter,

2002). This is in line with Hart (1998, p. 13) who stated that "experiences of inspiration contained each of these four dimensions [opened, energy, clarity and connectedness]. They help to identify (define) an experience of inspiration".

As this type of construct includes reflective as well as formative measures, we applied a mix of scale development techniques. In following the C-OAR-SE procedure (Rossiter, 2002, 2011), we attach particular importance to construct validity. This includes the identification of the scope of the constructs as well as the indicator specification. In addition, domain sampling is applied for the reflectively measured constructs (Bollen & Lennox, 1991; Rossiter, 2002). For the assessment of the formative model, we followed guidelines that meet the special requirements for these models (Diamantopoulos & Winklhofer, 2001; Hair, Black, Babin, & Anderson, 2010; Marko Sarstedt, Hair, Hwa, Becker, & Ringle, 2019). The overall index construction consists of qualitative and quantitative studies. In order to develop and validate the model of customer inspiration, theoretical and statistical criteria were used. Table 2.1 summarizes the various steps of the procedure.

Table 2.1 Overview of Index development procedure

No	Step	Task/Method	Assessment
Part 1: Measurement Model Development			
1	Literature review	Attribute & Item identification	Content validity
2	Focus groups	Attribute & Item generation	Content validity
3	Qualitative study	Item generation	Content validity
4	Validation interviews	Item translation	Content validity
		Item evaluation	Dimensionality
Part 2: Measurement Model Validation			
5	Main-study	Correlations	Discriminant power
		Exploratory factor analysis	Dimensionality
		Confirmatory factor analysis	Convergent validity
		Structural equation modeling	Discriminant validity
6	Validation study	Correlations	External validity

The index development procedure consists of two parts, namely the model development and the model validation parts, which can be further divided into six steps. Within Part 1, the main objective is to validate the content of the construct under investigation and to assess dimensionality. Content validation as "the degree to which elements of an assessment instrument are relevant to and representative of the targeted construct for a particular assessment purpose" (Haynes, Richard, & Kubany, 1995, p. 239) is of high importance when a new construct is developed, because it is the most essential validity type (Rossiter, 2002). Part 1 is particularly important for an index construction because it defines the entire scope of the construct that is covered by the measurement (Diamantopoulos & Winklhofer, 2001).

The model development contains four related steps. Step 1 is a literature review to identify attributes and items of related constructs that play a role within the conceptualization of customer inspiration (section 2.3.1). In Step 2, focus group interviews are conducted to capture the consumer perspective on how moments of customer inspiration are perceived by individuals, and to generate attributes and items based on these findings. In addition to the focus groups, a qualitative study was conducted in Step 3 to assess the consumer perspective on the construct facets. In Step 4, validation interviews helped to translate the items and to evaluate their clarity and coherence.

In Part 2 we attempted to validate the model and to empirically test the construct validity of customer inspiration (Diamantopoulos & Winklhofer, 2001). It is divided into two steps, starting with a main-study that first tested the discriminant power of all items. By means of an exploratory factor analysis we assessed the dimensionality of the scale and streamlined the item battery from 30 to final nine items. Confirmatory factor analysis helped to assess the model fit. In the final step, we assessed the external validity of the scale. Therefore, we conducted a second study which tested the final nine-item scale and linked it to an external variable for a final validation of the developed measurement model (Diamantopoulos & Winklhofer, 2001).

2.4   Index Development

2.4.1 Part 1: Model Development—Qualitative Approach

2.4.1.1 Literature Review
A detailed literature review of related work on inspiration (Hart, 1998; Oleynick et al., 2014; Shiota, Thrash, Danvers, & Dombrowski, 2014; Thrash & Elliot,

2003, 2004; Thrash, Maruskin, et al., 2010; Winterich et al., 2019), customer inspiration (Böttger et al., 2017; Rauschnabel et al., 2019), and charismatic and transformational leadership (Bycio, Hackett, & Allen, 1995; Conger & Kanungo, 1992) as well as on related constructs such as consumer engagement (Vivek et al., 2014), brand attachment (Park et al., 2010; Thomson et al., 2005), "aha" experiences (Skaar & Reber, 2020), and customer identification (Ahearne et al., 2005) revealed several potential attributes of customer inspiration. For instance, Hart (1998, p. 7) studied the "experience of inspiration in ordinary persons" and came up with four characteristics of inspirational experiences. As customer inspiration has similarities to the phenomena of charismatic or transformational leadership, additional attributes were deducted from this field. As described in section 2.3.1, customer inspiration has similarities to other constructs, such as self-brand connection or "aha" experiences, which were also screened for attribute and indicator identification. This step revealed several attributes and indicators on the emotional, cognitive or behavioral levels which are summarized in Appendix 3 within the Electronic Supplementary Material.

2.4.1.2 Focus Groups

In order to evaluate customer inspiration from the consumer perspective, focus group interviews were conducted.

Design

The aim of the focus groups was to identify how consumers experience the moment of inspiration. Various question techniques were applied to uncover these insights. Each focus group started with a general discussion about advertising, which included presenting various advertisements from different companies to the participants and asking their opinion about them. This procedure aimed to create a feel-good atmosphere that is important to get the most unbiased information from the focus group participants (Vence, 2005). Afterwards, the discussion was funneled towards the topic of inspirational brands. Participants were asked how they experienced an inspirational brand or moment and what triggered this experience. They were asked to write the answers down first, before sharing the results with the group.

Next, customer inspiration attributes that were derived from the literature review were presented to the participants. By means of a sorting task, participants had to evaluate these attributes regarding their relative occurrence within an inspirational moment. The results were discussed in plenum. Appendix 4 within the Electronic Supplementary Material presents an overview of the focus group discussion guide and of the group activities.

Sample

Eight consumers participated in two focus groups.[1] A detailed overview of the focus group participants of the two sessions is provided in Appendix 5 within the Electronic Supplementary Material. The participants were recruited by means of personal contact, word-of-mouth communication, and online postings on social media platforms (Facebook and Instagram). Participants were between 25 and 43 years old (M: 31.4, SD: 6.1). Three were female and five were male. There was no special requirement needed for participating in the focus group.

Analysis and Interpretation

The focus group interviews lasted between 60 and 90 minutes. They were all recorded and transcribed afterwards. Since the interviews were held in German, the text analysis was also done in German, before the results were translated into English. The transcribed text as well as the writing tasks of the focus group participants were analyzed using classic text analysis methods (e.g. Mayring & Fenzl, 2014). The most important information that needed to be deducted from the focus group interviews were attributes and items for the construct of customer inspiration. All participants mentioned an activating moment when being inspired by a brand or advertisement. This activation included actual behavior, like sharing information concerning the brand with others or researching the brand or topic which the brand addresses. Some participants also reported an inner impulse to react when being inspired by a brand or mentioned a high level of imagination. Although being inspired is a very personal experience which made it difficult to speak about, some participants opened up and reported an increased closeness to a given brand. This was also described as "being felt understood" by the brand. Some participants mentioned aspects of transformative ideas which caught their attention and which they translated into different behaviors. These behaviors were partly consumption oriented and partly not. In total, the analysis identified several attributes which can be subdivided into emotional (deep connection) attributes, behavioral (activation) attributes, and cognitive (personal insight) attributes. The main outcomes of the interview analysis are summarized in Table 2.2.

---

[1] Due to the COVID-19 crisis, no more focus groups could be conducted due to meeting restrictions. Therefore, the exercises, which worked well in the focus groups, were processed virtually by means of questionnaires. Details will be provided in the next chapter.

Table 2.2 Focus group interview results with exemplary statements

Aspect	Explanation	Statement Examples
Activation	Most of the participants mentioned an activating moment when being inspired by a brand or advertisement. This activation can be divided in three main sub dimensions: Firstly, it is about sharing the information with others or digging more deeply into the brand or topic for themselves. Secondly, participants mentioned an inner push to react to the advertising or the suggested situation of the brand. Thirdly, participants reported a high level of imagination on the product and the situation of using it.	*"Yeah, it kind of makes you think. Advertising isn't perceived as annoying but actually occupies you. I think it's different from other things. Especially if you think about it and deal with the topic even after you've seen the advertisement. You read more into the topic and think about the context of the product." (FG 1)* *"I really think about this product all the time, I research on the internet what I can do with it, what the others do with it, so I'm really active." (FG 1)* *"If it really appeals to me, it is mostly a fascination and also an increased motivation to pursue the topic or the product. And it definitely triggers me to want something, mostly the product that is described. For instance, when some skis are advertised and they throw themselves out of a helicopter in the advertisement, that I think I'm missing something in my life, sitting in the office." (FG 2)* *"And that you experience a bit of zest for action." (FG 2)*
Deep Connection	Some participants opened up and reported an increased closeness to the brand. This is often experienced as if they felt understood by the brand. Some participants also mentioned trust and believing in the brand as essential for inspiration.	*"The way I always experience inspiring advertising is that you take a step back. (…) I don't really buy it from influencers, but when user-generated content is displayed, I always think it's ok for people to do it, because they have done something with it themselves and want to show it. So how I experience inspiring advertising is above all authenticity and trust." (FG 2).* *"When I can empathize with the ad." (FG 2)* *"When I experience an advertisement as inspiring, then I get more sensitive and I notice when other people share it or talk about it..." (FG 1)*

(continued)

Table 2.2 (continued)

Aspect	Explanation	Statement Examples
Personal Insight	Some participants mentioned aspects of transformative ideas which caught their attention and which they translated into different behavior. This could be in the way they consume but also the way they live.	*"The trend over the last 10/20 years has been "Geiz is Geil", cheap and disposable society and then I just buy something new, and that's the antipole to it, I think that's really cool. You just buy a pair of shoes, they simply last for 10 years, you can always go back to the shop and it will simply be repaired again and you get an espresso. The brand inspires with sustainability and being handmade." (FG 2)* *"I find this simplicity and clarity so good. This minimalistic approach, as in my apartment. There must be little, clear lines; I like white, bright colors. (...) I rather believe in the philosophy of Steve Jobs. He constantly said "Simplify, simplify, simplify". And that's how he took the product in another direction." (FG 2)* *"And then there's the Mammut brand, which inspires me to go to the mountains and has been with me there for years. It's more of an outdoor story in that case." (FG 2)*

Note: FG = Focus group

As a last step, the focus group participants received a set of attributes written on cards. The cards differed between the first and second focus group due to the fact that outcomes from the first session were incorporated into the second session. Across both groups, emotion, motivation, and ideas were mentioned as critical components of an experience of customer inspiration. Additionally, energy, connection, and vision were mentioned by almost all participants as being components of customer inspiration. Insight, clarity, activation, and transformation were mentioned only occasionally. The results are shown in Appendix 6 within the Electronic Supplementary Material.

After the focus group sessions, attributes and items for customer inspiration were extracted from the interviews. All data from the interviews was screened a second time to extract a list of all facets of customer inspiration. We applied a more inclusive approach to the analysis to not exclude important aspects during this attribute and item generation phase.

2.4.1.3 Qualitative Study

Design

In addition to the focus groups, a qualitative online study was conducted to capture the consumer perspective on inspirational customer moments. Although an online survey does not encompass the full advantages of a focus group in terms of information gathering, the online study delivered further insights on a larger scale without personally meeting the participants. Online questionnaires have also been used in other studies for scale development purposes (e.g., Festge & Schwaiger, 2007; Skaar & Reber, 2020). We designed the survey based on the focus group sessions and adapted it to meet the online requirements. After a short introduction, participants were asked to think about an inspiring brand experience. We also asked the participants to mention an inspiring brand. This was followed by open questions regarding the reasons why they were inspired by their mentioned brand, and what this moment triggered in them. Next, indicators identified from previous studies (focus groups and literature review) were presented to the participants in a randomized order. Each indicator had to be evaluated based on whether it describes an inspirational moment or not. Afterwards, we asked the participants again to reflect on an experience of inspiration relating to brands, and to write down their thoughts. The full interview guide is shown in Table 2.3.

Sample

The survey was conducted using the online tool Qualtrics. The survey was placed on Amazon's crowdsourcing platform Mechanical Turk (MTurk) in order to recruit participants for the study, i.e. convenience sampling was applied. The platform is used in various studies for recruiting study participants (Goodman, Cryder, & Cheema, 2013). MTurk makes it possible to find participants from all over the world in a very short timeframe. A total of 30 participants (MTurkers) were asked to fill out the survey (HIT). The incentive for each HIT was set at USD 0.80. After the survey was conducted, respondents that completed the survey were compensated.

The answers from respondents who did not complete the questionnaire as instructed (i.e. who placed advertisements instead of answering the questions) were eliminated from the data set. Five out of the 30 participants had to be excluded from the data set because a first data screening showed abusive content. The age range of the respondents was between 18 and 69 (M: 35.2, SD: 11.5) with 21 male and 4 female participants.

Table 2.3 Interview guide—Qualitative study

Introduction	Welcome, general information, contact details
Briefing	Please think about a brand for a moment that **inspired you**—A brand that you maybe recently discovered or that has been by your side already for a long time. Important is, that this brand really inspired you. **Take your time (2 minutes) to think about this brand, the moment of inspiration and how you experienced this moment.**
Question 1	Now, think again about this brand that really inspired you. **Please describe in written words, what it was about the brand that inspired you.**
Question 2	**Please describe in written words, how you experienced the moment of inspiration triggered by the brand.** (*e.g. How did you feel? What did you experience? Did something change? What did you think?*)
Question 3	Now, think again about the moment when a brand really inspired you. **Please indicate which of the following statements would match to this moment of inspiration by a brand.** (*multiple answers possible*)

- I want to share the message with others.
- I want to learn more about the brand.
- I see the brand as a role model.
- I feel a certain anticipation for the product.
- My motivation goes up.
- I feel an inner push to do something.
- I feel enthusiastic about the brand or product.
- I imagine what I can do with the product.
- I see myself in the situation.
- I want the product so that I can implement the suggested.
- I think to miss something if I don't follow the suggested.
- I have to think about the brand for a long time.
- I am more involved with the brand than before.
- I feel touched by the advertisement.
- I feel connected with the brand.
- I have the feeling of coming home.
- I am passionate about the brand.

- I feel excitement about the brand.
- I trust the brand.
- I feel friendly about the brand.
- I believe in the brand.
- My perspective opens for moments in everyday life.
- My sight became clear.
- Everything feels alive.
- I feel present.
- The ad or product gives me food for thought.
- I think about the general message that goes beyond the product.
- I am encouraged to express my ideas and opinions.
- My priorities are rearranging.
- The brand shows me what is really important for me to consider.
- The brand excites me with its vision of what I could be able to accomplish if I follow the role model.
- The brand gives me sense of overall purpose.
- I look at things in new ways.
- None of the above

Question 4	Now, having read all these statements, are there other things that come into your mind, how you would describe **the moment of inspiration triggered by the brand.**
Demographics	Age, gender, residence, educational level

Analysis and Interpretation

All data generated from the open questions was analyzed and coded, again using classic text analysis methods (Mayring & Fenzl, 2014). The evaluation of the already generated indicators was based on quantitative analysis. When asked how the participants experience an inspirational brand or advertising, some of them reported an aroused state (e.g. "I feel invigorated" or "I feel energized"). Another common theme was the state of happiness that participants reported when describing their inspirational brand experience ("I feel good" and "I was happy" or "I felt very happy to view that brand"). Participants also mentioned that they want to spend more time with the brand and that they feel close to the brand. After the evaluation of the indicators, participants were again asked whether any additional aspects came to their minds regarding the experience of inspiration. Some respondents stated that they identify with the brand ("The brand reflects my style" or "The brand attracts me") and that the usage of an inspirational brand gives them a good, "enthusiastic" feeling. Some of the statements were: "It's like a new awakening and a big discover (sic) about things you had no idea you could accomplish" or "get strength to stand and rise again" or "make sense, very realistic". Table 2.4 gives an overview about the outcomes of the qualitative study. The analysis of the qualitative study resulted in eight additional items.

Table 2.4 Qualitative survey—Results

Aspects	Explanation	Statement Examples
Well-Being, Feel Good & Happiness	More than one third of all participants mentioned a positive emotion that they connect with the experience of inspiration. This positive feeling resulted either from seeing the advertising or brand or from using it and spending time with the brand.	*"I felt good and I was happy"* *"I feel (…) very happy. Yes, something changed."* *"Very pleasurable. I felt very happy to see that brand. That brand was very creative and made [me] hopeful."* *"I feel happy and I like to use this brand."* *"I feel awesome about the brand."*
Energy & Motivation	Some participants mention a shift in energy or motivational boost when they described an inspirational experience.	*"When I used the product, I felt invigorated. I felt a surge of energy."* *"I feel very fresh. Its experience is very nice. I think about this brand as motivation (sic) to me."* *"I felt little bit depressed at this very precise moment of my life; I saw a documentary about the brand and after I saw it, I felt energized."*

(continued)

Table 2.4 (continued)

Aspects	Explanation	Statement Examples
Spending Time with the brand & Closeness	Some participants reported a boost in the amount of dedicated time with the brand. Inspirational customer experiences result in a higher amount of time spent with the brand. This results in a greater proximity to the brand. In addition, proximity to the brand was also generally mentioned as a sign of customer inspiration.	*"I felt so great when I saw celebrities wearing the brand I like, thinking we are together and feeling attached to the star. It makes me feel to get more of clothing (sic) from the brand."* *"I watched a documentary one day on Steve Jobs on YouTube. It went over the history of Apple and how it was started. I've watched a lot of videos since then on Apple and have enjoyed learning about it."* *"It makes me feel to get more of clothing materials from the brand"*

2.4.1.4 Validation Interviews

For further evaluation of the items, validation interviews were conducted with student researchers in the field of business administration, as well as with consumers. The starting point were 66 items deducted from the literature review, the focus groups and the qualitative online survey that covered the construct of customer inspiration up to that point.

Before the interviews were conducted, the items had to be translated into German. The translation was done by a group of five working students that spoke both languages, German and English, fluently. One of the working students was a native English speaker. The translators were briefed to translate the item list from English to German. In the next step, an iterative back translation was conducted, and the results compared and discussed afterwards. This collaborative and iterative translation process followed the suggestions by Douglas and Craig (2007). The five working students also assessed whether there were any duplicates in the list of items. The outcome was a reduced list of 40 items in English and German.

The main objective of the interviews was to assess the overall clarity and completeness of each item in order to minimize response or other non-sampling errors (Assael & Keon, 1982). Each interviewee was presented with the item list and each of the 40 items was discussed. These cognitive interviews encouraged the respondents to think about the questions out loud and to comment on them to make sure that the items were properly understood (R. N. Bolton, 1993; Rossiter, 2002). Each respondent had to first indicate whether he/she understood the item and whether another phrasing would be more appropriate. Respondents were also asked if any items were missing. For this task, consumers were the target group of the interviews. We selected five consumers by means of convenience sampling for the validation interviews. Among the five interviewees were three working students and two professionals.

An additional task was to assign the items to the attributes in order to identify potential second-order dimensions and to assess the right level of abstraction. With the help of a sorting task, where indicators had to be assigned to the corresponding attributes of the construct, indicator validity can be assured (Anderson & Gerbing, 1991; Henseler, 2017). Respondents were given the final item list and were asked to assign these items to the attribute list discussed in the previous chapter. They were also asked to bundle items and to find new keywords for the bundles. This task was done with consumers[2].

Summary of Part 1
The aim of the steps in Part 1 was to capture all facets of moments of customer inspiration. Attributes and corresponding items were identified for measuring the construct. In the literature overview, existing elements of components regarding inspiration along the three themes of deep connection, personal insight, and activation were gathered. In two focus group interviews, the consumer perspective on customer inspiration was assembled. A qualitative survey added additional consumer statements which resulted in 66 items. This preliminary item list was translated and checked for duplicates by five working students before the reduced list of 40 items was assessed for clarity and appropriateness by means of validation interviews. The final result (see Appendix 7 within the Electronic Supplementary Material) is a list of 30 items that describe the facets of inspiration bundled under three attributes, namely activation, deep connection and personal insight. Based on the findings of Part 1, the classification based on the C-OAR-SE procedure (section 2.3.2) could be confirmed.

2.4.2 Part 2: Model Validation—Quantitative Approach

2.4.2.1 Main-Study
The first step of Part 2, the model validation, started with an empirical study. It was conducted with three main objectives in mind. Firstly, we wanted to assess whether the set of 30 items had enough discriminant power to distinguish between

---

[2] This task was performed with the help of a Master's student as part of her thesis under instruction of the author of this study.

an inspirational and a rather neutral brand (Engelmann, 2006). Secondly, we aimed to streamline the list of 30 items without losing any important aspects of the construct that was covered by the items (Diamantopoulos & Winklhofer, 2001; Schwaiger, 2004). Thirdly, we wanted to assess the dimensionality of the index and to validate the construct in terms of discriminant and convergent validity. For this endeavor, we conducted a paired sample t-test, exploratory factor analysis and confirmatory factor analysis. Additionally, we explored which brands are perceived as inspirational and which as rather neutral.

Survey Design

The study was conducted by means of an online survey using the tool Qualtrics. The study language was German. Participants were asked to think about a moment when they had been inspired by a brand. Participants had to name the brand which inspired them, and to evaluate it using the 30 customer inspiration items on a 7-point-Likert scale. Beforehand, a filter question sorted out participants that were not suited for filling out the survey by asking "Have you ever been inspired by a brand?". Respondents that answered this question with "yes" could continue with the survey, while respondents that answered "no" were directed to the demographics section at the end. With this filter question, we eliminated the respondents that were not familiar with an experience of inspiration. This approach has been used in similar studies (e.g. Skaar & Reber, 2020). Afterwards, we asked participants to think about a brand from the same category that had rather a neutral effect on them and which the participants do not perceive as "inspiring". This second brand should be named and evaluated along the 30 items as well. A demographics section concluded the survey.

Data Collection and Sample

The survey was distributed to a mailing list owned by the *Institute for Market-based Management* which includes mainly university alumni. In total, 3,000 people received the invitation to take part in the survey by E-Mail. The survey was also posted on social media platforms (Facebook and Xing). Overall, convenience sampling was applied. As an incentive, survey respondents were given the chance to win one of three vouchers (worth €20) for an online shop. In total, we received a response of 531 questionnaires, of which a large number contained missing data. We list-wise excluded questionnaires that were not fully completed and kept 285 questionnaires for further analysis. The data set comprised 161 female (56.5%), 121 male (42.5%) and 3 diverse (1.1%) respondents that were between 21 and 76 years old (M: 32.23; SD: 9.77). A total of 156 (54.3%) participants passed the filter question. There was no significant difference in terms of age or gender among the participants that passed the filter question. As each questionnaire included the evaluation of two brands (inspirational and neutral brand), we extracted a final number of 312 data sets (brand evaluations) for further analysis. As the minimal amount for each item to be tested is ten (M. Sarstedt & Mooi, 2014), the number of data sets was sufficient.

Discriminant Power and Correlations
We tested whether the set of items had the power to discriminate between the inspirational and the neutral brand. We chose the paired sample t-test as parametric test for comparing means among the two dependent observational groups. The t-test results showed that each of the 30 pairs of items differ significantly between both groups (p < .01). Next, we calculated Pearson correlations among all 30 items. The correlation analysis revealed that all correlations were above > .400 and statistically significant at p < .01 (Table 2.5).

Exploratory Factor Analysis
We performed exploratory factor analysis to understand the structure of the data and to streamline the item battery as we wanted to reduce potential information redundancies. We used principal component analysis with varimax rotation. The data was suitable for factor analysis with a Kaiser-Meyer-Olkin index of .976 and a significant Bartlett's Test of Sphericity ($\chi^2_{435} = 9164.56$, $p < .01$). All communalities were above .500 (Min = .590; Max = .825) after the extraction of three factors that together explained 70.92% of total variance. Two factors had Eigenvalues >1.000, and one factor had an Eigenvalue of .974. We choose the three-factor solution as our conceptualization also consisted of three components.

Factor 1 included items of the theme *deep connection* that reflected the emotional component of the construct. Item 7 "I feel enthusiastic about the brand", which was originally labeled as activation item, was assigned to the deep connection component. It seemed that the emotional meaning of the item prevailed the activating aspect. Factor 2 contained items of the theme *personal insight* that represented the cognitive component. Factor 3 carried items of the theme *activation* that constituted the behavioral component. Item 22 "The brand makes everything feel alive", which was originally labeled as personal insight item, was allocated to the activation theme. This assignment was carried out as factor 2 had now a clear transformational character whereas factor 3 contained the "energized" items. We named factor 1 *connection*, factor 2 *transformation* and factor 3 *activation*. All factors represent first-order components that were measured reflectively. Table 2.6 summarized the results of the exploratory factor analysis.

Table 2.5 Item correlations and descriptive statistics

	1	2	3	4	5	6	7	8	9	10	11	12	13	14	15	16	17	18	19	20	21	22	23	24	25	26	27	28	29	30
1	1																													
2	.713	1																												
3	.574	.670	1																											
4	.621	.613	.603	1																										
5	.650	.677	.641	.691	1																									
6	.600	.670	.607	.539	.732	1																								
7	.604	.716	.648	.601	.679	.781	1																							
8	.570	.614	.648	.714	.716	.640	.656	1																						
9	.624	.627	.543	.574	.633	.656	.671	.566	1																					
10	.606	.657	.591	.554	.641	.692	.638	.567	.579	1																				
11	.586	.697	.721	.707	.655	.697	.734	.705	.635	.665	1																			
12	.558	.558	.532	.540	.633	.609	.515	.612	.574	.556	.566	1																		
13	.670	.631	.536	.611	.621	.486	.471	.559	.458	.546	.524	.534	1																	
14	.729	.711	.575	.600	.656	.625	.597	.558	.588	.607	.610	.567	.742	1																
15	.722	.794	.641	.609	.680	.640	.642	.625	.549	.628	.638	.621	.685	.705	1															
16	.629	.691	.646	.603	.668	.706	.684	.650	.593	.642	.673	.629	.590	.664	.694	1														
17	.676	.721	.665	.613	.738	.779	.794	.692	.675	.607	.704	.632	.547	.684	.675	.741	1													
18	.633	.690	.679	.578	.660	.672	.777	.641	.654	.595	.678	.513	.526	.582	.608	.646	.753	1												
19	.585	.576	.648	.503	.664	.633	.597	.634	.577	.563	.592	.638	.504	.581	.578	.669	.724	.634	1											
20	.676	.725	.699	.656	.725	.765	.789	.701	.676	.697	.752	.625	.587	.696	.683	.752	.817	.783	.727	1										
21	.549	.504	.488	.587	.553	.453	.427	.525	.417	.509	.517	.523	.632	.594	.553	.488	.501	.436	.501	.499	1									
22	.567	.621	.587	.586	.750	.702	.615	.646	.602	.623	.654	.630	.550	.585	.578	.648	.662	.591	.677	.673	.548	1								
23	.626	.631	.588	.668	.553	.497	.548	.565	.463	.628	.621	.454	.627	.623	.596	.571	.582	.557	.503	.622	.664	.528	1							
24	.632	.636	.623	.589	.579	.499	.554	.551	.466	.537	.618	.451	.572	.615	.659	.593	.580	.544	.510	.602	.560	.537	.681	1						
25	.621	.541	.538	.619	.609	.442	.439	.563	.424	.523	.514	.521	.639	.597	.584	.591	.523	.457	.571	.571	.552	.619	.550	.661	1					
26	.569	.555	.570	.616	.640	.518	.498	.602	.457	.511	.531	.551	.611	.571	.593	.588	.549	.503	.566	.561	.619	.550	.625	.619	.618	1				
27	.582	.526	.550	.586	.586	.464	.493	.581	.447	.425	.537	.419	.588	.542	.519	.499	.578	.511	.530	.554	.655	.541	.545	.590	.561	.630	1			
28	.663	.739	.732	.665	.703	.738	.770	.672	.634	.692	.753	.606	.576	.664	.728	.735	.805	.742	.644	.795	.571	.585	.677	.569	.553	.589	.540	1		
29	.447	.505	.548	.489	.578	.502	.432	.561	.420	.485	.539	.544	.567	.510	.511	.609	.530	.462	.588	.547	.578	.617	.492	.641	.541	.603	.540	.540	1	
30	.620	.587	.581	.621	.596	.544	.530	.610	.454	.630	.574	.534	.650	.610	.639	.623	.593	.530	.576	.595	.705	.548	.742	.628	.643	.725	.634	.641	.557	1
M	3.12	3.28	3.02	3.01	2.76	3.08	3.68	2.79	3.13	3.13	3.09	2.20	2.59	2.77	2.99	2.92	2.99	3.35	2.23	2.95	2.54	2.43	3.14	3.36	2.54	2.56	2.84	3.16	2.08	2.91
SD	2.01	1.94	1.95	2.00	1.87	1.95	1.85	2.11	1.95	1.95	1.97	1.57	1.68	1.78	1.89	1.89	2.00	1.97	1.68	1.98	1.73	1.69	1.90	2.02	1.73	1.71	1.91	2.12	1.57	1.84

Note: All correlations are significant $< .01$, $N = 312$

In order to select the right number of items within each subscale, several aspects were taken into account. As domain sampling and parsimony are both important (Cronbach & Meehl, 1955; Hinkin, 1995; Rossiter, 2002), we wanted to ensure that all themes were reflected in the items and that unnecessary items were excluded. Furthermore, we wanted to create a simple structure but not to lose any explanatory power of the scale. For factor 1, we excluded items that showed lowest factor loadings (item 15 and 16). We kept item 17 ("I feel connected to the brand.") instead of items 18 ("I believe in the brand.") as the former was a more distinct item for the overall factor. For factor 2, we excluded the items with the lowest factor loadings (item 24, 25 and 26). For factor 3, we kept the items with the higher factor loadings (item 5, 8 and 22). Item 12 ("I miss out on something when I do not follow what the brand is demonstrating.") was eliminated from factor 3 as we wanted to design a coherent subscale. Compared to the other items, item 12 did not fit into the overall scale very well due to its length.

Table 2.6 Results of exploratory factor analysis after varimax rotation

No	Items	Factor 1	Factor 2	Factor 3
Activation				
1	I want to talk about the brand with other people.	.564	.610	.130
2	I want to find out more about the brand.	.706	.502	.125
3	The brand promotes norms and values, which leads me to perceive it as a role model.	.604	.413	.318
4	For me, the brand creates the urge to act.	.468	.577	.294
5	When I think of the brand I feel full of energy.	.590	.389	**.495**
6	Thinking of the brand, I experience anticipation.	.774	.192	.375
7	I feel enthusiastic about the brand.	**.842**	.247	.192
8	The brand makes me ready to take on new challenges.	.543	.372	**.497**
9	I envision what I am able to do with the brand.	.714	.211	.275
10	The brand stimulates my imagination.	.633	.424	.202
11	I want to realize what the brand is presenting to me.	.698	.377	.289

(continued)

Table 2.6 (continued)

No	Items	Factor 1	Factor 2	Factor 3
12	I miss out on something when I do not follow what the brand is demonstrating.	.462	.279	(.582)
Deep Connection				
13	I need to spend a long time thinking about the brand.	.311	.722	.271
14	I need to think about the brand frequently.	.538	.604	.190
15	I want to engage more with the brand.	(.593)	.576	.181
16	I feel emotionally touched by the brand.	(.632)	.383	.399
17	I feel connected to the brand.	**.764**	.305	.358
18	I believe in the brand.	(.773)	.288	.218
19	The brand is a part of me.	.531	.263	.600
20	I identify with the brand.	**.774**	.344	.328
Personal Insight				
21	Through the brand I experience sudden realizations.	.157	**.710**	.421
22	The brand makes everything feel alive.	.524	.292	**.605**
23	The brand sets me thinking.	.383	**.764**	.128
24	I think about the message the brand is communicating.	.428	(.684)	.126
25	The brand makes me feel encouraged to voice my opinion.	.230	(.698)	.372
26	The brand makes me rearrange my priorities.	.241	(.635)	.490
27	The brand shows me what is truly important to me.	.262	.577	.434
28	The brand gets me enthusiastic about its vision.	.734	.436	.259
29	The brand makes me see a purpose in life.	.224	.391	.708
30	The brand makes me see things in a new way.	.304	**.726**	.343
Variance explained		32.17%	24.75%	14.00%

Note: Rotation converged in 12 iterations. Bolded factor loadings indicate which factor the item loaded into. Items of which the loadings are in brackets are excluded from the final scale.

At the end, each subscale consisted of 3 items. This is in line with the findings of Rossiter (2002, p. 317), who proposes that for eliciting attributes each attribute should be represented by items of "reasonable" amount in order to reflect the state adequately. This approach resulted in a simpler and more manageable structure of the scale, with three distinct factors, one representing the *connection* theme, one the *personal insight* theme, and one focusing on the *activation* theme. We performed the exploratory factor analysis a second time with the remaining 9 items (Table 2.7). The three factors explained 83.27% of the total variance. All communalities were between .710 and .860. The factor loadings were all above .500 (Min = .540; Max = .857). We proceeded with the nine-item solution for further analysis.

Table 2.7 Results of exploratory factor analysis after varimax rotation of final nine items

Item		Factor 1: Connection	Factor 2: Transformation	Factor 3: Activation
5	When I think of the brand I feel full of energy.	.503	.298	**.705**
7	I feel enthusiastic about the brand.	**.857**	.225	.276
8	The brand makes me ready to take on new challenges.	.546	.352	**.540**
17	I feel connected to the brand.	**.790**	.294	.375
20	I identify with the brand.	**.792**	.320	.355
21	Through the brand I experience sudden realizations.	.085	**.811**	.420
22	The brand makes everything feel alive.	.365	.278	**.805**
23	The brand sets me thinking.	.426	**.807**	.109
30	The brand makes me see things in a new way.	.337	**.810**	.247
Variance explained		*33.00%*	*27.71%*	*22.55%*

Note: Rotation converged in 12 iterations. Bolded factor loadings indicate which factor the item loaded into.

Confirmatory Factor Analysis
We applied confirmatory factor analysis to assess the factor structure and its goodness-of-fit using the covariance-based structural equation modeling tool AMOS 26. We chose the most common fit indices that were suggested by prior research for model fit evaluation including model chi-square (χ^2), comparative fit

index (CFI), and root mean square error of approximation (RMSEA) (Carmines & Mciver, 1981; Hair et al., 2010). Our model indicated a good overall fit (χ^2_{24} = 41.297, p < .015, χ^2/df = 1.721, CFI = .992, RMSEA = .048) meeting conventional guidelines (Barrett, 2007; Bentler & Bonett, 1980; Zinnbauer & Eberl, 2005).

In order to assess the convergent validity of the three subscales we analyzed factor loadings, squared multiple correlations, corrected item-total correlations, average variance extracted (AVE), and construct reliability (CR). All factor loadings were statistically significant and had factor loadings of above .700. Squared multiple correlations were between .628 and .827 and corrected item-total correlations between .730 and .852. AVE should be above .500, which was the case for the factors *connection* and *transformation* (.661/.655). The factor *activation* had a slightly lower AVE of .479. CR was at .854 for *connection*, .851 for *transformation* and at .729 for *activation*, indicating the reliability of the construct as the values were above the threshold of .700 (Hair et al., 2010). Cronbach's alpha values for all three constructs indicated internal reliability for *connection* (α = .923), *transformation* (α = .876), and *activation* (α = .876) (Nunnally, 1978).

Discriminant validity was tested in two ways. Firstly, we compared the AVE for *connection* (AVE = .661), *transformation* (AVE = .655) and *activation* (AVE = .479) with the squared correlations between the constructs. The AVE should be higher than the squared correlation (Fornell & Larcker, 1981) which was not the case for the factors *connection* and *activation*. Secondly, we assessed cross-loadings as the "item-level discriminant validity" (Henseler, Ringle, & Sarstedt, 2015, p. 118). We again evaluated the results of the exploratory factor analysis. Apart from one exception (item 8), all items loaded more strongly on the factor to which they were theoretically assigned to, and showed no cross-loadings which is in favor of acceptable discriminant validity (Henseler et al., 2015). Based on these results, we could not obtain a clear result with regard to discriminant validity. This issue will be further explored in the discussion section. Besides this fact and the slightly lower AVE of factor 3, the results show a good fit of the model and are in favor of convergent validity among all items. Table 2.8 summarizes all results.

Our last objective was to get a better picture of which brands are perceived as inspiring and which as being rather neutral. Table 2.9 shows the top 5 brands in each category. Nike and Adidas, two sports and apparel brands, appear in both categories. Among the inspirational brands, Apple and two automotive brands, BMW and Tesla, were mentioned. Among the rather neutral brands, Puma, Esprit and H&M were named most often.

Table 2.8 Results of confirmatory factor analysis

Items	Corrected Item-total Correlation	Standard-ized Factor Loadings	Squared Multiple Correlations
Connection	$\alpha = .923$, CR $= .854$, AVE $= .661$		
I feel enthusiastic about the brand.	.830	.865	.748
I feel connected to the brand.	.852	.909	.827
I identify with the brand.	.847	.907	.824
Transformation	$\alpha = .876$, CR $= .851$, AVE $= .655$		
Through the brand I experience sudden realizations.	.733	.793	.628
The brand sets me thinking.	.762	.841	.708
The brand makes me see things in a new way.	.794	.884	.781
Activation	$\alpha = .876$, CR $= .729$, AVE $= .479$		
When I think of the brand I feel full of energy.	.807	.885	.783
The brand makes me ready to take on new challenges.	.730	.822	.675
The brand makes everything feel alive.	.754	.817	.667
Global Fit Statistics	$\chi 2 = 41.297$, df $= 24$, $\chi 2/df = 1.721$; p $= .015$; RMSEA $= .048$; CFI $= .992$		

Note: $\alpha =$ Cronbach's alpha; CR $=$ Construct reliability; AVE $=$ Average variance extracted; CFI $=$ Comparative fit index; RMSEA $=$ Root mean square error of approximation.

Table 2.9 Top 5 Inspirational and neutral brands (N $= 156$)

Inspirational	Rather neutral
Nike (10), Apple (7), Adidas (4), BMW (4), Tesla (3)	Adidas (12), Nike (9), Puma (7), Esprit (5), H&M (4)

2.4.2.2 External Validity

As a final step, we assessed the external validity of customer inspiration by linking the construct to an outcome variable (Diamantopoulos & Winklhofer, 2001; Hair et al., 2010). Previous studies about customer inspiration provided evidence that the construct drives customer loyalty, satisfaction, and impulse buying behavior (Böttger et al., 2017). Customer brand loyalty is a fundamental concept in marketing research and practice (Khamitov et al., 2019) that's why many studies are dedicated to identify its drivers (e.g. Khamitov et al., 2019; Palmatier, Dant, Grewal, & Evans, 2006; G. Watson et al., 2015). A meta-analytical study of customer-brand relationship constructs, such as brand attachment (Park et al., 2010), brand love (Carroll & Ahuvia, 2006), or self-brand connection (Escalas & Bettman, 2003) found that "love-based and attachment-based brand relationships are most strongly linked to customer brand loyalty" (Khamitov et al., 2019, p. 450). Since customer inspiration is also characterized by a close self-brand connection that is part of the brand attachment construct (Park et al., 2010), we hypothesize that customers who indicate a higher level of customer inspiration towards a brand also show a higher loyalty towards the brand. Based on this hypothesis, both components of customer inspiration should be positively correlated with brand loyalty.

Study Design

In order to assess external validity, we created a fresh data set by means of an online survey which was programmed with the tool Qualtrics. The study language was English. We applied convenience sampling by using the crowdsourcing platform Amazon Mechanical Turk (MTurk) to recruit survey participants and oriented ourselves along the approach used for previous studies (e.g. Skaar & Reber, 2020; Tucker, 2015). Although this platform faces some criticism, especially with regard to data quality, it provides great advantages as long as suitable precautions for its usage are taken into account (Cheung, Burns, Sinclair, & Sliter, 2017; Hunt & Scheetz, 2019; Kees, Berry, Burton, & Sheehan, 2017). One strategy that we applied to mitigate potential data quality issues was the application of a second platform provider, CloudResearch. This provider uses MTurk as a data source, but adds additional barriers and data quality checks on top of it. The basic handling is similar to using MTurk directly. In addition, only participants (MTurkers) who have completed more than 100 high intensity tasks (HITs) with an approval rate of over 90% were allowed to respond to the survey. Each survey was one HIT. The incentive was set at USD 0.80 per HIT.

The survey started with a short introduction. Afterwards, all respondents were confronted with a video advertisement of Nike, a well-known sports and apparel brand. We pre-selected this brand based on our previous findings about inspirational brands (section 2.4.2.1). After watching the advertisement, respondents had to rate the nine items of customer inspiration and answer questions regarding their loyalty towards the brand. For measuring brand loyalty, respondents had to answer two questions on a 7-point-Likert scale that we took from Thomson et al.

(2005) (Table 2.10). We received a response of 144 filled out questionnaires. In the sample, 46.5% of all participants were female and 53.5% were male. The average age was 41.17 (SD: 12.04).

Analysis and Results
We started the analysis with an exploratory factor analysis and saved the factor scores for subsequent analysis. The extracted three-factor solution explained 91.86% of total variance. Communalities were all above .700. The factor loadings were all between .299 and .859. Next, we computed correlations between all three items that measure brand loyalty and the factor scores of the three subconstructs of customer inspiration using SPSS. Table 2.10 shows the results. The variables correspond to the predictions made above and are positively correlated at a significance level of $p < .01$. These results are in favor of the external validity of the construct.

Table 2.10 Correlations between constructs and brand loyalty items

	Connection	Transformation	Activation
Brand Loyalty			
How would you characterize your loyalty toward this brand ?	.562**	.267**	.455**
How does this brand compare to your 'ideal' brand?	.672**	.368**	.311**

Note: ** $p < .01$, N= 144

2.5   Discussion

Marketing researchers and practitioners are constantly searching for ways to attract consumers and turn them into loyal fans (Umashankar, Ward, & Dahl, 2017; Yim, Tse, & Chan, 2008). One promising strategy could be to inspire consumers by touching their soul, creating enthusiasm, and transforming their thoughts. Although inspiration is mainly discussed in the psychological domain (Oleynick et al., 2014; Thrash, Elliot, et al., 2010), first studies have started to examine customer inspiration, its conceptualization, antecedents, and consequences in the marketing context. The prevailing opinion sees customer inspiration as a two-factor construct with an *inspired-by* and *inspired-to* component (Böttger et al., 2017; Thrash & Elliot, 2003). However, their two-factorial view does not take into account all facets of inspiration (**Study I**). Inspired customers tend to be more loyal, satisfied, and prone to impulse buying (Böttger et al., 2017). A customer's state of inspiration can even explain a higher level of intention to recycle in the context of product transformation salience (Winterich et al., 2019). The authors of these studies are important pioneers for establishing customer inspiration in the marketing literature, but there is still a long way to go to explore the full potential of customer inspiration for marketing and to better understand its importance for theory and practice.

With this study, we took a first step in this direction, and tried to expand the knowledge about this construct. We provide a tool to measure customer inspiration, which we define as the level of identification with a brand and the activation through the brand. Our purpose was to develop a theoretically and conceptually well-founded measurement model of customer inspiration for scientific purposes and for marketing practitioners. Based on a thoroughly developed definition of customer inspiration, which was deducted from expert knowledge (**Study I**), an index was constructed following the C-OAR-SE procedure (Rossiter, 2002). In the first part of the study, we conducted several tasks to uncover all aspects of the construct and focused on its content validity. We spoke with consumers to uncover their thoughts on inspirational experiences with brands and interviewed experts to evaluate the generated items. The second part of the study emphasized construct validity. By means of two empirical studies we refined, assessed, and validated the index of customer inspiration. This resulted in a type II measurement specification that identifies customer inspiration as a formative second-order construct of three reflective first-order components (Jarvis et al., 2003).

Based on our theoretical foundation, we assumed a three-component model as we identified three themes that specify a moment of customer inspiration, namely *activation, deep connection,* and *personal insight.* The exploratory factor analysis detected as well three dimensions within the data set. We named the first factor (or first-order construct) *connection* as it included items of the *deep connection* theme. The second factor was named *transformation* and it contained mainly personal insight items. We slightly modified the name of the second factor, as the transformative character became increasingly apparent during the discussions with focus group participants and experts in the validation interviews. The third factor was named *activation.* The final customer inspiration measurement model consists of nine items, of which three items each measure *connection, transformation,* and *activation.* All items represent a statement that is to be rated on a 7-point-Likert scale. Since customer inspiration is rated by individuals (consumers) (Rossiter, 2002), the statements are also formulated from their perspective. Together, they form the customer inspiration index.

Within the overall index development procedure, we applied several techniques to meet the requirements for a reliable and valid measuring instrument. In general, we followed the C-OAR-SE procedure (Rossiter, 2002) by putting special emphasis on the model development phase to assure content validity of the construct. Expert interviews formed the basis for the definition of the construct and its conceptualization. A subsequent literature review analyzed analogies between the findings from the interviews and the established constructs which substantiated the conceptualization. Focus group sessions and a qualitative study added the consumer's perspective to construct specification. The outcome of the above mentioned approach was a set of 30 items. From here, we deviated from the procedure proposed by Rossiter (2002, 2011) and followed the suggestions made by Diamantopoulos (2005) and Diamantopoulos and Winklhofer (2001). As a result, we applied multivariate data analysis methods to reduce the number of items from 30 items to finally nine. A final correlation analysis with items that measure a hypothesized outcome variable, brand loyalty, confirming external validity was performed, and a first attempt to uncover the constructs the nomological network was made.

Our findings have implications for both, theory and practice. We add to the existing research stream on customer inspiration and provide a different conceptualization of the construct compared to the prevailing opinion in literature. With this study we show that customer inspiration is made up of three components, *connection, transformation,* and *activation.* All three components are required to determine a moment of customer inspiration. In contrast to the existing conceptualization by Böttger et al. (2017), our conceptualization is more inclusive and takes inspiration through brands outside the purchase environment into account. Further, we incorporated an emotional component into the scope of the construct and emphasized the transformational character thereof. We see the construct of Böttger et al. (2017) as a more narrow concept that sets buying impulses or provides ideas regarding how to combine products in a new way. Within our understanding, customer inspiration sets impulses for transformative thinking that can lead to purchase behavior, but most importantly also creates value for the consumer as it provides impulses and inspiration for daily life. With this study, we also add to the stream of research of customer-brand relationships (Fetscherin & Heinrich, 2015; Khamitov et al., 2019), as we understand customer inspiration as a form of a customer-brand relationship (Fournier, 1998). Similar to the relationship of a charismatic leader with his followers, inspiration links brands to consumers. The brand is a source of guidance that transforms the values and aspirations of consumers, who thus identify with the brand.

For practitioners, we provide a clear understanding of the concept customer inspiration that is usually rather complex and hard to grasp. Since our results are based on expert knowledge, the results are fundamentally connected with practice. With our tool, marketing departments can measure the level of customer inspiration evoked by brands. Since many companies measure and monitor brand equity on a regular basis, the nine-item measure can be incorporated in overall brand equity studies (e.g., Kantar, 2020). In addition, similarly to the Prophet Brand Relevance Index®, brands across companies or industries can be compared by building a customer inspiration index score. To do this, an average score of each component has to be calculated (Rossiter, 2002). Agencies can use our tool to assess customer inspiration indices within their brand tracking studies and to extend their service portfolio.

Limitations and Directions for Further Research
Apart from the findings for theory and practice, this study also comes with some limitations. Firstly, although we provide a theoretically substantiated and parsimonious measure that helps marketing researchers to assess customer inspiration with nine items which can be easily incorporated into other studies, we do not address the question of what really drives customer inspiration. In order to be able to build inspiring brands and marketing tools that inspire, it is important to know which approach should be taken to create inspirational content and brands. Therefore, future work should focus on the identification of the drivers of customer inspiration.

Secondly, within the assessment of discriminant validity, we obtained conflicting results. As the Fornell-Larcker criterion was not fulfilled, the validity of the two factors, *connection* and *activation*, and consequently of the overall construct, was questionable (Fornell & Larcker, 1981). As discriminant validity assures that the "construct measure is empirically unique and represents phenomena of interest that other measures in a structural equation model do not capture" (Henseler et al., 2015, p. 116), one potential explanation could be the formative nature of *connection, transformation,* and *activation*. In literature, there is a lack of agreement regarding how discriminant validity for a formative measurement can be evidenced. Based on Diamantopoulos and Winklhofer (2001), "classic" construct validity assessment in terms of convergent and discriminant validity cannot be applied. However, the authors refer to formative indicators instead of second-order formed constructs. In contrast, Jarvis et al. (2003) underline the assessment of discriminant validity of formative models. We follow the argumentation of Jarvis et al. (2003), and see other potential explanations for the result. It may stem from distracted or inattentive respondents and fast-clickers that did not take enough time to answer the survey questions with attention. As a consequence, the data set did not capture the full variance of all items. Future work could address this points by adding additional attention checks, to ensure better data quality. Future work should also take different validation methods using PLS-SEM into account (Marko Sarstedt et al., 2019).

Thirdly, in all three of our empirical studies, we assessed inspirational brands, either by self-elicitation of the brand or by choosing the brand Nike. In contrast, within two studies we asked for rather neutral brands, which should actually have been from the same category. Consequently, only product categories that include inspiring brands were evaluated. Due to this, we cannot conclude that customer inspiration is applicable for every product type. Our pre-study revealed that sports, apparel, and automotive brands were mentioned as inspirational brands. Although this study does not deliver enough information to draw a final conclusion, one might think that customer inspiration may only be applicable for hedonic or image brands (Dhar & Wertenbroch, 2000). We think that this is not the case, but future work should find evidence for the generalizability of customer inspiration. Research could potentially be conducted on the question regarding for which product types customer inspiration has the biggest leverage. In addition to the product type, consumer traits which are more accessible for inspirational brands than others, could also be analyzed.

Fourthly, in Step 6, we analyzed correlations between brand loyalty items and each factor of the model. Although this procedure allows us to draw conclusions about the external validity, we neglected the higher-order structure of the model (Marko Sarstedt et al., 2019). Our approach represents a simplified testing procedure, but it could contain statistical inaccuracies. This could have been avoided by using the repeated indicator approach using the PLS-SEM (Hair et al., 2014). Future work should address this shortcoming and use structural equation modeling to map the overall structure of the model customer inspiration.

Study III: The Explanatory Power of Customer Inspiration

Abstract

Market researchers and practitioners are constantly searching for explanations for consumers' decision-making, brand preferences, and brand choices. The role of brand attitude and its importance for the understanding of consumer behavior is well established. In this context, a growing body of research explores the role of customer-brand relationships. Customer inspiration is a fairly new construct among these relationship constructs and it still lacks verification of its theoretical and practical value, including in relation to other constructs. This study tries to fill this gap and compares the explanatory power of the newly-developed customer inspiration construct, the established construct of brand attitude, and customer inspiration conceptualized by Böttger et al. (2017). Within two studies, we investigated which construct better explains the willingness to pay a price premium and purchase intention. The results provide evidence that customer inspiration offers value over brand attitude and customer inspiration by Böttger et al. (2017) in predicting both outcome variables. With these findings, we could indicate that it is worthwhile for practitioners to invest in activities that inspire customers, besides creating a positive attitude towards the brand. In addition, we provide evidence that our conceptualization and measurement of customer inspiration is a better predictor than the existing measure of Böttger et al. (2017).

Supplementary Information The online version contains supplementary material available at (https://doi.org/10.1007/978-3-658-35894-5_3).

3.1   Motivation

The COVID-19 pandemic is affecting markets and consumers (Galoni et al., 2020). Since one country after the other went into lockdown in 2020, a large part of the economy was in a kind of rigidity for weeks. This reality—which many people had never experienced before—developed a threat to consumers' income and quality of life (Campbell et al., 2020). Some industries—like the fashion industry—were hit especially hard by the crisis since the demand for non-essential products dramatically decreased (Bianchi et al., 2020). Overall, the crisis pressured markets and raised the price-sensitivity of consumers (Abdelnour, Babbitz, & Moss, 2020). These uncertain times challenge companies in addition to the already-increased market pressure that has resulted from higher switching rates and lower attention spans of consumers (Kotler, Kartajaya, Setiawan, & Pyka, 2017; Wirtz, 2001). Consequently, businesses have to adapt their marketing strategies to the new requirements (Bianchi et al., 2020). For instance, a major strategy consulting firm predicts less consumer spending overall, higher preferences for either lower-priced goods or premium brands that deliver additional value, higher demand for sustainable and purposeful brands, and consumers' expectation for relevant messages and shopping experiences for fashion brands (Bianchi et al., 2020). How should brand and marketing managers respond to this forecast? Marketing departments certainly need to allocate scarce resources to winning strategies and activities to "create and communicate value to customers to drive their satisfaction, loyalty and profitability" (Kumar & Reinartz, 2016, p. 36). In operational terms, companies need to identify and manage suitable marketing metrics that deliver the highest return and long-term success.

One central metric is brand equity, which is defined as "outcomes that accrue to a product with its brand name compared with those that would accrue if the same product did not have the brand name" (Ailawadi, Neslin, & Lehmann, 2003, p. 1). Key dimensions of brand equity are brand awareness and brand associations (Keller & Lehmann, 2006). It determines how much customers are willing to pay for a product (Aaker, 1996). Especially in competitive markets, brands are valuable intangible assets for companies to stand out from other companies (Wood, 2000). However, what role do brands play within a crisis? The market research company Ipsos assumes that "emotional closeness and identifying with the personal goals, values and circumstances of consumers will play an even more prominent role in impacting brand choice" (Dumouchel & Kahn, 2020, p. 4). According to their study, brand closeness will further grow as a brand equity driver in contrast to brand performance.

This debate about close relationships between customers and brands has also captured the attention of marketing scholars (Fetscherin & Heinrich, 2015). Since the pioneering work on consumer-brand connections by Fournier (1998), research on customer-brand relationships has become quite popular, leading to a whole new research stream around customer-brand relationships (Fetscherin & Heinrich, 2015). Among these are phenomena like brand love (Batra et al., 2012), self-brand connection (Escalas & Bettman, 2003), and brand attachment (Park et al., 2013), which can have a positive effect on key performance indicators like customer brand loyalty (Khamitov et al., 2019), the willingness to pay for a brand (Batra et al., 2012), or purchase behavior (Park et al., 2010). Nguyen and Feng (2020) even analyzed the broader financial impacts of brand love, finding that it drives firm profitability and market value in the long term, especially for hedonic brands. The effect is stronger for brands that operate in highly competitive markets. However, the question emerges whether such theoretical models have a higher predictive power for consumer behavior than classic "plain vanilla" constructs such as brand attitude (Shimp, 1981; Udell, 1965), which is one of the core variables in theory (Park & Macinnis, 2006) as well as practice (Rossiter, 2014).

In addition to the aforementioned consumer-brand relationship constructs, an additional construct, customer inspiration (Böttger et al., 2017), comes into play. Customer inspiration defined as the level of identification with and activation through a brand's mindset and actions (**Study I**) is another customer-brand relationship construct. It could be an important success factor for brands to create loyal customers and achieve a higher willingness to pay, especially in a market environment that has an "increased demand for purpose-driven brands" and that searches for additional value from brands (Bianchi et al., 2020). With its psychological roots (Hart, 1998; Thrash & Elliot, 2003), marketing studies have picked up the construct in the shopping environment and found evidence that this phenomenon is a valuable driver of customer satisfaction, positive affect, and impulse buying (Böttger et al., 2017). However, literature about customer inspiration is still scarce. Further, only little research has been made until now about the comparison of brand attitude and customer-relationship constructs in terms of "usefulness" and explanatory power. One of the few are Park et al. (2010) who conceptually and empirically distinguished brand attachment and brand attitude strength. They found that brand attachment does add value as a construct of interest in marketing and practice by providing evidence that brand attachment is a better predictor of actual pro-brand behavior than brand attitude strength.

This study ad hand tries to add to this research stream by targeting three main objectives. Firstly, this study sheds light on the explanatory power of customer inspiration as conceptualized in **Study I** and **II** towards market relevant outcome variables. Secondly, this study compares the explanatory power and predictive relevance of customer inspiration against brand attitude. Thirdly, this study contrasts the two conceptualizations of customer inspiration in terms of explanatory power and predictive relevance.

This study strives to answer the question whether customer inspiration represents a key variable that drives marketing success, in terms of willingness to pay a price premium and purchase intention. Based on this endeavor, the following research questions arise:

RQ1: How does the level of customer inspiration affect willingness to pay a price premium and purchase intention?

RQ2: How does the level of involvement with the product determine the impact of customer inspiration?

RQ3: Which of the three predictor variables of customer inspiration, brand attitude, and customer inspiration by Böttger et al. (2017) has a higher explanatory power toward willingness to pay a price premium and purchase intention?

In order to answer these questions we conducted two empirical studies. Both studies are based on an online survey. We compared the two conceptualizations of customer inspiration and brand attitude by examining how well each of the three constructs predict other relevant outcome measures. Within a first study, we assessed a well-known sports and fashion brand. The second study aimed to replicate the findings of the first study and examined a brand from the automotive industry. We used variance-based structural equation modeling to estimate our models by means of the program SmartPLS (Ringle, Wende, & Becker, 2015) and utilized SPSS for subsequent analyses.

The remainder of this study is structured as follows. First, we provide the theoretical background of the most relevant constructs under study, which will lead to the conceptual framework of this study, including the derivation of our hypotheses. Subsequently, each empirical study will be described in detail, followed by its data analysis and results. Implications for practice and future research possibilities will conclude this study.

3.2   Literature Review and Hypotheses

3.2.1 Why Consumers are Willing to Pay a Higher Price

Although technological enhancements have raised market transparency, which enables consumers to compare prices in easier ways (Rossi & Chintagunta, 2016), situations where consumers are less price-sensitive and are willing to invest in certain products still exist (Ailawadi et al., 2003). Consumers' willingness to pay a price premium for their preferred brand over another brand of the same quality and size can be seen as a summary measure of brand equity (Aaker, 1996). In general, willingness to pay a price premium is defined as the maximum amount of money that an individual is willing to invest in a product or service (Koschate-Fischer, Stefan, & Hoyer, 2012) and it describes a measure of preference (O'Donnell & Evers, 2019). It results from well-managed consumer-based brand equity facets like perceived quality, perceived value for the cost, and brand uniqueness (Keller, 1993; Netemeyer et al., 2004). Accordingly, this is why consumers are willing to pay more for e.g. national brands compared with private labels (Steenkamp, Van Heerde, & Geyskens, 2010). Besides the perceived quality of a product (Netemeyer et al., 2004), several other drivers of consumers' acceptance of paying a higher price have been identified. Whereas brand awareness is a prerequisite (Aaker, 1996), a well-managed brand experience that additionally underlines the brand credibility and perceived uniqueness of a brand creates the effect that consumers are willing to pay more (Dwivedi, Nayeem, & Murshed, 2018). Further, social image and home country origin explain a higher willingness to pay a price premium (Anselmsson, Bondesson, & Johansson, 2014) and the list can be continued almost infinitely since it is a measure of brand strength overall (Aaker, 1996; Keller, 2001; Netemeyer et al., 2004). From a company perspective, a higher willingness to pay a price premium is desirable because it leads to more flexibility in pricing. Overall, when consumers are willing to pay a price premium, revenues increase and higher margins can be realized (Stahl, Heitmann, Lehmann, & Neslin, 2012). The luxury industry in particular makes use of this advantage when only a "happy few" can afford certain products to signal their status (Dion & Borraz, 2017, p. 67). However, other companies like food brands also benefit from consumers who are willing to pay a certain price premium for a certain brand that evokes rational as well as emotional sentiments and delivers a desirable social image (Anselmsson et al., 2014).

3.2.2 The Explanatory Power of Customer Inspiration

Research about customer inspiration and its explanatory power remains scarce. The first studies provide evidence that the construct can explain consumer behavior, emotions, and attitudes (Böttger et al., 2017). Positive affect, transcendent customer experience, and customer delight were identified as emotional consequences, customer satisfaction and loyalty intention as attitudinal and impulse buying as behavioral consequences (Böttger et al., 2017). A detailed examination of a second-order construct revealed that the two components inspired-by and inspired-to correlate differently depending on the respective construct. Customer delight and transcendent customer experience more strongly correlate with the inspired-by component and impulse buying more strongly with the inspired-to component. On the other hand, positive affect correlates equally strongly with each component (Böttger et al., 2017). Further, a study conducted within the online shopping context revealed that customer inspiration has a significant influence on the number of clicks, products viewed, shopping duration, and purchase intentions (Böttger et al., 2017). The authors argue that the inspired-by component is more related to general exploration behavior as part of the deliberation phase of the decision journey, whereas the inspired-to component is more related to product-specific exploration behavior and marks the transition to the implementation phase of decision-making. Böttger et al. (2017) also found a positive effect on purchase likelihood of customer inspiration as part of a repeated study within the field setting.

However, these findings refer to the conceptualization of customer inspiration by Böttger et al. (2017), which differs in essential elements from the construct that is the focus of this study. As mentioned earlier, consumer-based brand equity facets serve as key indicators for a willingness to pay a price premium (Netemeyer et al., 2004). Among these brand equity facets are brand awareness (Cobb-Walgren, Ruble, & Donthu, 2013), brand associations (Keller, 1993), brand image (Sharp, 1995), as well as brand relationships (Keller, 2001). Hence, brands that are able to form relationships with their consumers can charge a price premium. This is in line with empirical findings by Thomson et al. (2005) who identified emotional brand attachment as an indicator for willingness to pay a price premium. Since customer inspiration not only comprises a connection between a customer and the brand that results in a customer-brand relationship but also incorporates a transformational component that might add additional value to the customer, we hypothesize the following:

H1a: Customers who show a higher level of customer inspiration towards a brand have a higher willingness to pay a price premium for the brand.

Besides a higher willingness to pay a price premium, consumer-based brand equity dimensions can also result in higher purchase intentions (Cobb-Walgren et al., 2013). Through emotional branding-evoked inspiration, consumers' brands "become part of their life stories, memories, and an important link in their social networks" (Thompson, Rindfleisch, & Arsel, 2006, p. 51). Hence, inspired customers who are tied to a brand in this very special way should also show a higher purchase intention (Keller, 1993). In addition, inspired customers share certain aspects with engaged consumers (Brodie, Ilic, Juric, & Hollebeek, 2013; Pansari & Kumar, 2017).[1] Engaged consumers who interact with brands also show a higher purchase intention compared with non-engaged consumers (Prentice, Han, Hua, & Hu, 2019). In sum, special connections between customers and brands seem to evoke a higher intention to buy the brand. We therefore hypothesize the following:

H1b: Customers who show a higher level of customer inspiration towards a brand have higher purchase intention for the brand.

The Interplay of Customer Inspiration and Involvement

Involvement is often used to explain different advertising responses (Kim, Baek, & Choi, 2012). Depending on the involvement level of consumers, ads can be perceived differently and purchase intentions can vary (Kim et al., 2012; R. E. Petty, Cacioppo, & Schumann, 1983; Steenkamp et al., 2010). Batra and Stephens (1994, p. 199) argue that "moods and emotions appear to influence brand attitudes more in low personal relevance (…) situations than under high-motivation conditions". The distinction between low- and high-involvement products (e.g., R. E. Petty et al., 1983; Rossiter & Percy, 1985) refers to the level of search and conviction level required to make the purchase decision and it is based on the economic theory by Nelson (1970). Back then, brands primarily fulfilled the risk reduction function as consumers were not as informed about product information as nowadays (Kapferer, 2008; Swaminathan et al., 2020). In general, involvement can refer to a product, issue or a response (R. E. Petty et al., 1983). We use the term to reflect a consumer's enthusiasm and feelings of interest towards a product (Goldsmith & Emmert, 1991). Involvement is characterized by the perceived personal relevance (Celsi & Olson, 1988), which occurs when an individual's

---

[1] A detailed comparison between customer inspiration and customer engagement can be found in **Study I**.

needs, goals, and values can be linked with the product. Product characteristics that match personal goals and values appear relevant (Celsi & Olson, 1988). Therefore, the involvement classification always applies to a particular product or brand and a particular audience or person (Rossiter & Percy, 1985). The moment of inspiration for a customer is characterized as an identification with the brand. We think that this identification should be easier to achieve for a product that is perceived as a high-involvement product and consequently with a higher personal relevance for a consumer. Therefore, we argue that the level of involvement with the product moderates the effect of customer inspiration. Hence, we hypothesize the following:

> H_{2a}: *Involvement with the product moderates the effect of customer inspiration on willingness to pay a price premium in the sense that the more involved that a customer is with the product, the higher the willingness to pay a price premium.*

> H_{2b}: *Involvement with the product moderates the effect of customer inspiration on purchase intention in the sense that the more involved that a customer is with the product, the higher the purchase intention.*

3.2.3 Customer Inspiration Versus Brand Attitude

In this study, we want to compare the explanatory power of customer inspiration and brand attitude. Brand attitude can be defined as a "buyer's evaluation of the brand with respect to its expected capability to deliver on a currently relevant buying motive" (Rossiter, 2014, p. 537) and thus it represents a special form of the general attitude as defined by Ajzen and Fishbein (1977). Brand attitude is a relatively "enduring, unidimensional summary evaluation of the brand that presumably energizes behavior" (Spears & Singh, 2004, p. 55). Definitions and conceptualizations of (brand) attitudes are vast and widely differ, ranging from single attitude models to meta-cognitive models (R. Petty, Briñol, & Demarree, 2007). The majority of these definitions share in common the notion that attitude is centered or directed to an object and that it has an evaluative nature (Giner-Sorolla, 1999). Within the advertising communication model by Rossiter and Percy (1985), brand attitude represents one of the five basic communication effects that advertising tries to shape. These five effects include (1) a consumer's category need, (2) the consumer's awareness of the brand, (3) at least a rather favorable attitude towards the brand, (4) an intent to buy, and ultimately (5) the

purchase facilitation. Rossiter and Percy (1985, p. 512) argue that brand attitude "consists of an (…) affective motivation-related component which energizes
brand choice and a (…) cognitive belief component which directs choice toward
the particular brand".

Customer inspiration and brand attitude have similarities. Both constructs are
of a psychological nature and refer to a brand, and both incorporate an assessment
either of the evaluative object or the connection between the customer and the
brand. Both are multidimensional, comprising cognitive, affective, and behavioral
components (Ajzen, 1988), when considering the tripartite view of brand attitude
(Park & Macinnis, 2006). As explanatory variables, both constructs have effects
on consumer behavior, in case of brand attitude on brand purchase, repeat purchase, and willingness to recommend a brand (Park et al., 2010) and in case
of customer inspiration on customer loyalty and impulse buying (Böttger et al.,
2017).

Besides these similarities, they also differentiate in certain aspects. For
instance, customer inspiration and brand attitude differ in the type of effect
that they create. Although potentially favorable, brand attitude reflects a rather
"cold" affection (Park & Macinnis, 2006; Thomson et al., 2005). By contrast,
customer inspiration has a rather "warm" character, reflected in the deep connection between customers and brands represented by the *connection* component. In
addition, brand attitude reflects an individual's evaluation of a brand that is relatively enduring (Linda Hollebeek, 2011b). Customer inspiration appears rather
sudden and in a rush, similar to "aha" experiences (Skaar & Reber, 2020). Further,
customer inspiration activates the consumer to think and enables transformative thinking. It further activates consumers to follow new ideas and approaches,
which makes customer inspiration much more "activating" than the conative component of brand attitude (**Study I**). To summarize the discussion above, customer
inspiration shares similarities and elements with brand attitude but goes beyond
the evaluative construct due to its activating and transformational character.

3.2.4 The Role of Brand Attitude in Marketing Research

Brand attitude is one of the central constructs in marketing (He, Chen, & Alden,
2016). A large number of studies exist on how brand attitudes are formed (e.g.
Yoo & MacInnis, 2005), how they change (e.g. Hoch, 2002; Lutz, 1975), and
what effects they have on consumer behavior (e.g. Park et al., 2010; Spears &
Singh, 2004). Based on the theory of planned behavior by Ajzen (1985), attitudes play a major role when it comes to intentions and consequently actions.

The theory claims that humans form beliefs based on the available information from which attitudes, subjective norms and perceived behavioral control emerges. Based on these three elements, humans build intentions about certain behavior and consequently actual behavior (Ajzen, 1985). Hence, attitudes influence behavior through these behavioral intentions (Fishbein & Ajzen, 1975). However, the close relationship between attitude and behavior does not automatically make attitude a good predictor of behavior (Ajzen & Gilbert Cote, 2008). According to the MODE model by Fazio (1990), only strong attitudes that are accessible in people's memory can be a good predictor of specific behavior. Many studies analyzing the predictive power of brand attitude build on these findings by explicitly considering and measuring brand attitude strength (e.g. Eggert, Steinhoff, & Witte, 2019; Park et al., 2010; Priester, Nayakankuppam, Fleming, & Godek, 2004).

Brand attitude (strength) has been identified as a key antecedent for consumer behavior (Park et al., 2010). In a set of experiments, Priester et al. (2004) showed that attitude and attitude strength influence brand consideration. Consideration of a brand further mediates the effect of attitude strength on brand choice. Many studies have also shown that brand attitude is an important antecedent of purchase intention (Lutz, McKenzie, & Belch, 1983; MacKenzie, Lutz, & Belch, 1986). Brand cognitions—i.e. "recipients' perceptions of the brand being advertised"—cause these brand attitudes, which then affect purchase intentions (Lutz et al., 1983, p. 533). Purchase intentions are "an individual's conscious plan to make an effort to purchase a brand" (Spears & Singh, 2004, p. 56). Further, brand attitude acts as a mediator between attitude towards the advertisement (A_{Ad}) and purchase intentions (Ozer, Oyman, & Ugurhan, 2020). This relationship was also found in the research on A_{Ad} and brand choice. A study by Biehal, Stephens, and Curlo (1992) analyzed direct and indirect effects of A_{Ad} on brand choice and showed that brand attitude mediates the effect of A_{Ad} and brand choice. Table 3.1 summarizes the findings of the literature review.

An influencing factor of the predictive power of (brand) attitudes on behavior has been provided by the elaboration-consistency hypothesis of R. Petty et al. (1995). According to the theory, attitudes formed by a higher amount of issue-relevant thinking are better predictors of behavior than those resulting from more peripheral thinking. This applies for settled attitudes and newly-developed attitudes (R. Petty et al., 1995). The authors further provide examples of issue-relevant thinking and elaborating messages, e.g. in studies where respondents were instructed to make self-relevant connections (Shavitt & Brock, 1986) or when messages had more personal relevance (e.g. Leippe & Elkin, 1987). In line with the elaboration-consistency hypothesis are findings about moderators

Table 3.1 Overview of literature review

Antecedent	Mediator Variable	Consequence	Source
Attitude	Behavioral Intention	Actual Behavior	Fishbein and Ajzen (1975)
Attitude Strength		Purchase Behavior	Priester et al. (2004), R. Petty, Haugtvedt, and Smith (1995), Fazio (1995), Park et al. (2010)
Attitude Strength	Brand Commitment	True Brand Loyalty	Kim, Morris, and Swait (2008)
Attitude towards the Ad	/	Brand Attitude	Gardner (1985); Mitchell and Olson (1981)
Attitude towards the Ad	Brand Cognition	Brand Attitude	MacKenzie et al. (1986)
Attitude towards the Ad	Brand Attitude	Purchase intention	Lutz et al. (1983); Ozer et al. (2020); Spears and Singh (2004)
Attitude towards the Ad	Brand Attitude	Brand Choice	Biehal et al. (1992)

that affect the relationship between attitude and behavior. Among these are variables such as accessibility, extremity, and consistency that are associated with the issue-relevant elaboration, which moderate the attitude-behavior relation (R. Petty et al., 1995). This also explains the relatively higher predictive power of brand attitude strength compared with brand attitude (Park et al., 2010). In sum, brand attitude influences purchase intention, brand loyalty, and brand choice. Additionally, strong attitudes act as a better predictors for human behavior than attitudes overall (Fazio, 1990). Based on the elaboration-consistency hypothesis by Petty et al. (1995), attitudes based on issue-relevant thinking better predict behavior. Represented by the transformation component that contains "aha" experiences, transformational thoughts, and other meta-cognitive feelings, customer inspiration constitutes a moment of high elaboration towards the brand. Therefore, we hypothesize the following:

H_{3a}: Customer inspiration is a better predictor of a consumer's willingness to pay a price premium than brand attitude.

H_{3b}: Customer inspiration is a better predictor of a consumer's purchase intention than brand attitude.

3.2.5 Comparing two Measures of Customer Inspiration

Böttger et al. (2017, p. 117) define customer inspiration as "a customer's temporary motivational state that facilitates the transition from the reception of a marketing-induced idea to the intrinsic pursuit of a consumption-related goal". In our study, we use a different definition of customer inspiration. We see customer inspiration as "the intensity of an individual's identification with and activation through a brand's mindset and actions" (**Study I**). Each episode of customer inspiration includes cognitive, affective, and behavioral elements. The cognitive and affective elements of customer inspiration incorporate e.g. "aha" experiences, other meta-cognitive feelings as well as transformative thoughts of customers, and the behavioral element captures the activation of individuals, both within and outside the direct consumer-brand encounter. Customer inspiration further involves a strong emotional bond between the individual and a brand, also described as a deep connection that individuals form with organizations, based on personal experiences with the brand's mindset and actions.

In the conceptualization by Böttger et al. (2017), we identified an activation and insight component. Our conceptualization of customer inspiration contains three components, namely connection, transformation and activation. Both customer inspiration definitions and conceptualizations share common aspects, although the transformational character and the deep connection theme of our definition differentiate us from Böttger et al. (2017). Our definition is built from expert knowledge and takes into account the consumer perspective, whereby we think that our measure of customer inspiration is more precise and therefore also a better predictor of relevant outcome variables. Therefore, we hypothesize the following:

H_{4a}: *Customer inspiration is a better predictor of a consumer's willingness to pay a price premium than customer inspiration by Böttger et al. (2017).*

H_{4b}: *Customer inspiration is a better predictor of a consumer's purchase intention than customer inspiration by Böttger et al. (2017).*

The overall research model is depicted in Figure 3.1.

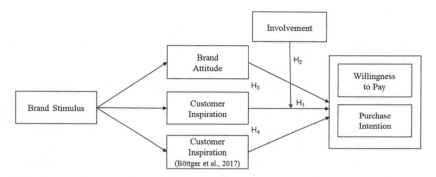

Figure 3.1 Research model and hypotheses

3.3   Study 1

3.3.1 Survey Design

The study was conducted as an online survey using the market research software Qualtrics. Convenience sampling was applied as survey respondents were recruited on the Amazon Mechanical Turk (Mturk) platform with the help of an intermediary service provider, CloudResearch (Goodman et al., 2013). All survey participants were exposed to a video advertisement of the well-known sports and apparel brand Nike. The video was part of the "Dream Crazy" campaign launched in 2018 (Nike, 2018). The brand and the video were pre-selected based on findings about customer inspiration in **Study II**.[2] The brand was also used within a study about brand attachment and brand attitude strength (Park et al., 2010). The survey started with a short introduction, after which all respondents were exposed to the advertisement and had to answer an attention check question that referred to the video advertisement. Next, all participants had to answer questions regarding their level of customer inspiration and their attitude towards the brand. We included also questions regarding their willingness to pay a price premium, purchase intention and product involvement. A set of control variables and questions about demographics completed the survey.

---

[2] In **Study II**, Nike was the most often mentioned brand when asking consumers about an inspiring brand.

3.3.2 Measures

Dependent Variables
In order to measure the willingness to pay a price premium, we followed the operationalization by Netemeyer et al. (2004) and selected a subset of two items from the overall four-item set. This selection has been done in a previous study by Warren, Batra, Loureiro, and Bagozzi (2019) and allowed us to keep the questionnaire as short as possible. We asked participants to rate the brand upon the two statements on a seven-point Likert scale, anchored from strongly disagree (1) to strongly agree (7).

For measuring purchase intention, we again followed the operationalization by Netemeyer et al. (2004) and asked the participants to rate a statement about their purchase intention on a seven-point Likert scale, anchored from strongly disagree (1) to strongly agree (7). Further, we included a question about their purchase likelihood, similar to the operationalization of Spears and Singh (2004), and asked the respondent to rate the statement on a seven-point Likert scale, anchored from would definitely not buy it (1) to would definitely buy it (7).

Explanatory Variables
For assessing the level of customer inspiration, we used the customer inspiration scale developed in **Study II**. The measure includes three factors, namely connection, activation and transformation. Each of the nine items overall had be rated on a seven-point Likert scale, anchored from strongly disagree (1) to strongly agree (7).

For the assessment of brand attitude, we followed the conceptualization of Park et al. (2010). We measured the attitude valence with three semantic differentials good/bad, pleasant/unpleasant, and like/dislike on a seven-point scale. In addition, respondents were asked to answer two additional questions that captured the extent to which they were confident and certain about their brand evaluation. The latter two items were a subset of the overall attitude strength conceptualization by Krosnick, Boninger, Chuang, Berent, and Carnot (1993). The selection of the two certainty/confidence items followed the approach of Park et al. (2010). Each item was rated on a seven-point Likert scale, anchored from not at all (1) to completely (7). Within our study, we mainly use attitude valence items to measure brand attitude, apart from a robustness analysis in which we compared customer inspiration with brand attitude strength.

For measuring the existing construct of customer inspiration by Böttger et al. (2017), we used their customer inspiration scale, which contained ten items to measure two components, inspired-by and inspired-to. Each of the ten items of the two-dimensional scale had be rated on a seven-point Likert scale, anchored from strongly disagree (1) to strongly agree (7).

For measuring involvement, a subset of the items introduced by Zaichkowsky (1985) was used. Respondents had to rate the brand on a seven-point semantic differential scale in terms of how important/unimportant, interesting/boring, relevant/irrelevant, meaningful/not meaningful, and useful/useless the brand is for them. The subset partly followed the selection by Thomson et al. (2005).

Control Variable

We included consumer-, brand-, and ad-specific characteristics in our study to account for potential influencing factors within the research model. For consumer-specific characteristics, we also included gender, age and income. For ad- and brand-specific characteristics, we included ad liking (Bergkvist & Rossiter, 2007) and brand familiarity (Campbell, Keller, Mick, & Hoyer, 2003). Table 3.2 provides an overview of variables and items included in the questionnaire.

Table 3.2 Variables, items, and source

Variable	Item	Code	Source
	Dependent Variables		
Willingness to Pay a Price Premium	Are you willing to pay more for Nike than for other brands in the same product category?	WP1	Netemeyer et al. (2004)
	Are you willing to pay a higher price for Nike than for other brands?	WP2	
Purchase Intention	For my next purchase of sports equipment, I intend to buy a Nike brand.	PI1	Netemeyer et al. (2004), Spears and Singh (2004)
	How likely is it that you would buy this brand (Nike)?	PI2	
	Explanatory Variables		
Customer Inspiration	I feel enthusiastic about the brand.	CI1	Study II
	I feel connected to the brand.	CI2	
	I identify with the brand.	CI3	
	Through the brand I experience sudden realizations.	CI4	
	The brand sets me thinking.	CI5	

(continued)

Table 3.2 (continued)

Variable	Item	Code	Source
	The brand makes me see things in a new way.	CI6	
	When I think of the brand I feel full of energy.	CI7	
	The brand makes me ready to take on new challenges.	CI8	
	The brand makes everything feel alive.	CI9	
Brand Attitude	Indicate how well one or the other adjective in each pair describes your overall feeling of Nike:		Krosnick et al. (1993), Park et al. (2010)
	Bad-Good	BA1	
	Pleasant-Unpleasant	BA2	
	Dislike-Like	BA3	
	How confident are you with your evaluation?	BC1	
	How certain are you with your evaluation?	BC2	
Customer Inspiration by Böttger et al. (2017)	My imagination was stimulated.	CB1	Böttger et al. (2017)
	I was intrigued by a new idea.	CB2	
	I unexpectedly and spontaneously got new ideas.	CB3	
	My horizon was broadened.	CB4	
	I discovered something new.	CB5	
	I was inspired to buy something.	CB6	
	I felt a desire to buy something.	CB7	
	My interest to buy something was increased.	CB8	
	I was motivated to buy something.	CB9	
	I felt an urge to buy something.	CB10	
Involvement	Indicate how well one or the other adjective in each pair describes what sport is for you:		Zaichkowsky (1985)
	Important-Unimportant	Iv1	
	Interesting-Boring	Iv2	

(continued)

Table 3.2   (continued)

Variable	Item	Code	Source
	Relevant-Irrelevant	Iv3	
	Meaningful-Not Meaningful	Iv4	
	Useful-Useless	Iv5	
Control Variables			
Ad Liking	Thinking about the ad for Nike which of the following statements best describes your feelings about the ad?	AL	Bergkvist and Rossiter (2007)
Brand Familiarity	How familiar are you with the brand Nike?	BF	Campbell et al. (2003)
Gender, Income, Age		G, In, A	NN

3.3.3 Analysis and Results

Descriptive Statistics
We received 144 completed surveys. The data set was modified by eliminating all respondents whose answers showed straight lining behavior (N = 34). In these cases, the respondents' answers showed no variance in their assessments of the focal constructs. After this exclusion, 110 surveys remained. 47.3% of the participants were female and 52.7% male. All participants were located in the United States. The sample size of 110 was in line with the minimum requirements proposed by Hair et al. (2014). The respondents were between 21 and 67 years old (M: 41.47, SD: 12.07). Appendix 1 within the Electronic Supplementary Material provides a detailed overview of the composition of the respondent sample. All other descriptive statistics are presented in Table 3.3.

Hypothesis Testing
The aim of the study was to expand the knowledge about the nomological network of customer inspiration as well as its relative explanatory power compared with established constructs, brand attitude and customer inspiration by Böttger et al. (2017). In addition, we examined potential influencing factors that may alter this relationship. In order to estimate our models and test our hypotheses, we used the variance-based partial least squares (PLS) method as a structural equation modeling (SEM) technique and worked with the tool SmartPLS 3.0 (Ringle et al., 2015).

Table 3.3 Correlations and descriptive statistics

Variable	1	2	3	4	5	6	7	8	9	10	11	12	13	14	15	16	17	18	19	20	21	22	23	24	25	26	27	28	29	30	31	32	33	34	35
1 WP1	1																																		
2 WP2	.980	1																																	
3 PI1	.867	.857	1																																
4 PI2	.837	.843	.886	1																															
5 CI1	.689	.651	.721	.728	1																														
6 CI2	.732	.720	.707	.712	.716	1																													
7 CI3	.799	.777	.756	.780	.742	.846	1																												
8 CI4	.649	.632	.589	.588	.573	.712	.668	1																											
9 CI5	.571	.552	.520	.570	.479	.685	.622	.673	1																										
10 CI6	.648	.656	.594	.593	.581	.772	.733	.738	.752	1																									
11 CI7	.684	.687	.658	.739	.720	.818	.746	.667	.694	.747	1																								
12 CI8	.769	.752	.712	.752	.740	.762	.793	.714	.710	.754	.829	1																							
13 CI9	.670	.680	.647	.685	.665	.795	.749	.718	.689	.770	.867	.812	1																						
14 BA1	.669	.645	.694	.719	.803	.633	.715	.448	.360	.514	.601	.643	.595	1																					
15 BA2	.500	.494	.525	.550	.564	.469	.518	.380	.305	.338	.445	.476	.408	.680	1																				
16 BA3	.677	.662	.689	.719	.811	.674	.706	.511	.444	.547	.627	.686	.671	.936	.618	1																			
17 BC1	.181	.140	.164	.095	.335	.149	.161	.171	.121	.059	.136	.113	.139	.211	.252	.155	1																		
18 BC2	.156	.137	.145	.082	.313	.163	.154	.184	.112	.094	.157	.120	.160	.198	.319	.128	.940	1																	
19 CB1	.488	.459	.476	.549	.573	.587	.543	.523	.685	.620	.589	.689	.606	.556	.334	.617	.041	.005	1																
20 CB2	.556	.541	.592	.583	.604	.605	.550	.590	.579	.574	.642	.669	.620	.530	.339	.599	.018	-.005	.729	1															
21 CB3	.640	.627	.599	.618	.534	.644	.610	.676	.651	.692	.688	.715	.694	.483	.333	.564	.039	.056	.659	.825	1														
22 CB4	.568	.554	.596	.628	.561	.677	.629	.606	.734	.669	.697	.742	.708	.569	.386	.613	.087	.079	.780	.733	.718	1													
23 CB5	.645	.653	.598	.623	.485	.658	.619	.616	.684	.645	.636	.653	.643	.468	.286	.550	.035	.015	.639	.709	.786	.754	1												
24 CB6	.632	.623	.651	.647	.563	.564	.583	.586	.482	.524	.565	.584	.536	.495	.337	.531	.158	.119	.496	.640	.619	.552	.606	1											
25 CB7	.633	.636	.642	.658	.541	.589	.586	.581	.534	.538	.591	.596	.582	.494	.324	.533	.151	.092	.515	.613	.608	.561	.641	.931	1										
26 CB8	.619	.618	.629	.669	.538	.571	.581	.543	.548	.499	.562	.573	.560	.504	.300	.581	.121	.049	.566	.604	.583	.608	.661	.881	.917	1									
27 CB9	.577	.574	.584	.618	.532	.541	.545	.528	.487	.486	.564	.578	.563	.488	.290	.537	.117	.050	.556	.647	.619	.559	.600	.889	.928	.896	1								
28 CB10	.578	.592	.553	.602	.498	.517	.524	.552	.489	.509	.530	.540	.523	.455	.280	.515	.105	.099	.499	.583	.612	.509	.609	.886	.933	.895	.921	1							
29 BF	.284	.278	.293	.250	.283	.235	.235	.249	.182	.170	.089	.159	.091	.179	.128	.230	.368	.320	.121	.155	.146	.179	.222	.263	.249	.273	.207	.239	1						
30 AL	.610	.612	.614	.643	.618	.621	.637	.570	.559	.546	.607	.616	.580	.631	.440	.687	.077	.082	.662	.602	.620	.631	.646	.569	.557	.602	.549	.547	.118	1					
31 Iv1	.178	.209	.166	.102	.032	.045	.144	.161	.066	.064	-.039	.028	.030	.029	.152	-.025	.220	.266	-.070	-.140	-.081	-.012	.029	.063	.019	.007	-.030	.012	.142	-.058	1				
32 Iv2	.230	.235	.239	.231	.185	.108	.234	.185	.129	.155	.089	.045	.084	.029	.067	.076	.157	.193	.171	.132	.117	.151	.337	.048							.691	1			
33 Iv3	.122	.164	.164	.125	.084	.090	.151	.216	.058	.107	-.011	.067	.048	.084	.137	.058	.148	.229	-.006	-.065	-.035	.082	.084	.100	.040	.049	.007	.090	.159	.116	.777	.613	1		
34 Iv4	.210	.252	.237	.235	.130	.153	.259	.241	.100	.164	.142	.181	.205	.093	.196	.055	.103	.178	.032	-.002	.062	.059	.084	.125	.101	.058	.107	.096	.068	.057	.743	.709	.782	1	
35 Iv5	.033	.084	.092	.076	.002	-.008	.054	.106	.044	.027	.007	.031	.063	.029	-.118	.031	.021	.025	-.006	-.030	.000	.009	.045	.031							.736	.560	.798	.737	1
M	3.49	3.44	3.8	4.07	4.65	3.80	3.95	3.69	4.25	4.04	4.13	4.24	3.99	5.32	5.14	5.36	6.07	6.06	4.45	3.85	3.31	4.20	3.60	2.92	2.95	3.10	3.05	2.85	6.07	4.00	4.62	5.03	4.95	4.85	5.59
SD	1.90	1.86	1.82	1.84	1.55	1.76	1.62	1.64	1.73	1.71	1.75	1.69	1.71	1.51	1.66	1.60	.96	1.01	1.71	1.70	1.60	1.80	1.67	1.73	1.72	1.74	1.76	1.65	1.12	1.11	1.56	1.38	1.56	1.59	1.32

Note: Significant correlations ($p < .05$) are in bold font; all variables could be rated on seven-point scale (Min = 1; Max = 7) except AL (Min = 1; Max = 5)

For the evaluation of the measurement model and its moderating effects, we followed the procedure by Hair et al. (2014). As customer inspiration and customer inspiration by Böttger et al. (2017) are higher-order constructs, we assessed them first and continued afterwards with the reflective measures. The assessment of the structural model concludes this section. Across all PLS model estimations, we used the path-weighting scheme for inside approximation to ensure well-predicted latent variable scores (Fornell & Cha, 1994). For the assessment of the significance of the path coefficients, we used a bootstrapping routine with 5,000 subsamples and an individual sign change option. In addition, we utilized SPSS for the subsequent analyses in which we compared ΔR^2 values depending on the respective predictor variable.

Assessment of the Higher-Order Constructs

As customer inspiration is a higher-order construct comprising the three components of connection, transformation, and activation, it was first necessary to assess the hierarchical components as part of our overall model (Ringle, Sarstedt, & Straub, 2012). We used the two-step approach to estimate the higher-order construct (Becker, Klein, & Wetzels, 2012; Hair et al., 2014; Marko Sarstedt et al., 2019). First, we applied the repeated indicator approach to assess the validity of the reflective measurement for the lower-order constructs (LOCs) and estimate the latent variable scores (LVSs) for the three LOCs. Within the second step, the three LVSs served as manifest variables for the higher-order construct (HOC). In order to check for criterion validity, we related the measurement model to the construct willingness to pay. The first stage started with the evaluation of the composite reliability, Cronbach's alpha values, loading levels, and the average variance-extracted (AVE) to assess internal consistency, indicator reliability and convergent validity of the reflective measurements for the three LOCs. For the assessment of discriminant validity, we chose the heterotrait-monotrait ratio of correlations (HTMT) (Henseler, Ringle, & Sarstedt, 2014). The HTMT$_{reference}$ values were all below the threshold of 1.0, which is a sign of discriminant validity. As the results indicated a satisfactory quality of the measurement of the LOCs (Table 3.4), we proceeded with the second stage of the hierarchical component model assessment.

Table 3.4 LOCs—Reflective measurement assessment

Construct	Items	Load-ing	C.R.[1]	Cron-bach's α	AVE	D.V.[2]?
LOC1: Connection	I feel enthusiastic about the brand.	.882***	.943	.909	.846	Yes
	I feel connected to the brand.	.935***				
	I identify with the brand.	.941***				
LOC2: Transforma-tion	Through the brand I experience sudden realizations.	.890***	.929	.886	.814	Yes
	The brand sets me thinking.	.892***				
	The brand makes me see things in a new way.	.924***				
LOC3: Activation	When I think of the brand I feel full of energy.	.952***	.961	.939	.891	Yes
	The brand makes me ready to take on new challenges.	.933***				
	The brand makes everything feel alive.	.946***				

Note: * p < .1; ** p < .05; *** p < .01; [1] Composite Reliability; [2] Discriminant Validity

In the second stage, we assessed the formative measurement of customer inspiration, and hence the relationship between the three LOCs with the HOC. The LOCs were replaced by the LVSs, which served as manifest indicators for customer inspiration. In order to assess this structure, we used the variance-inflation factor (VIF) to uncover potential collinearity issues (Hair et al., 2014). VIF values of connection and transformation were below 5, which indicated a rather low level of collinearity. The VIF of activation had a value of 5.702. As the value was still far below the less restrictive threshold of 10, we proceeded with our analysis (Hair et al., 2010; Hair et al., 2014). Next, we assessed the outer weights and outer loadings of the HOC. The results are shown in Table 3.5. The outer weights represent the indicators' relative contribution to the overall construct. All three showed positive values, although the outer weights of transformation and activation were not significant. In this case, special attention was dedicated to the outer loadings that represent the absolute contribution to the construct. Indicators that have values of outer loadings above .500 but non-significant outer weights can be interpreted as absolutely important but not relatively important (Hair et al., 2014). All outer loadings constituting the absolute contribution to the construct were high with values above .500 and significant. The results suggested that all three components are important for the customer inspiration construct in absolute terms.

Table 3.5 HOC—Formative measurement assessment

Indicator	VIF	Outer Weights	Outer Loadings
Connection	4.282	.701***	.987***
Transformation	3.613	.108 (NS)	.854***
Activation	5.702	.231 (NS)	.933***

Note: * p < .1; ** p < .05; *** p < .01

As a final step, we assessed the criterion validity of the customer inspiration construct by linking it to the exogenous construct of willingness to pay. We selected this construct as it is part of the overall model. For the analysis of the path model, we used the R^2 value, which showed a moderate value of .652. This result indicated that all three indicators are good predictors of willingness to pay. We additionally calculated the Stone-Geisser's Q^2 value, which is an indicator for predictive relevance by using a blindfolding procedure with an omission distance of seven. The resulting Q^2 value of .628 gave an acceptable value of the predictive relevance. In sum, the results were in favor of the validity of the customer inspiration construct.

As customer inspiration by Böttger et al. (2017) is another HOC in our model comprising an inspired-by and an inspired-to component, we proceeded with the assessment of its hierarchical structure following the same approach as before (Ringle et al., 2012). The results are indicated in Table 3.6. The HTMT$_{reference}$ values were all below the threshold of 1.0, which is a sign of discriminant validity. The results showed a satisfactory quality of the measurement of the LOCs and we could proceed with the second stage of the hierarchical component model assessment.

As customer inspiration by Böttger et al. (2017) is specified as reflective within the HOC, we assessed the LVSs with the same approach as we previously did with the reflective measures of the LOCs. The results were overall of satisfactory level and are presented in Table 3.7. The HTMT$_{reference}$ values were all below the threshold of 1.0, which is a sign of discriminant validity.

Table 3.6 LOCs—Reflective measurement assessment of CI by Böttger et al. (2017)

Construct	Items	Load-ing	C.R.[1]	Cron-bach's α	AVE	D.V.[2]
LOC1: Inspired-by	My imagination was stimulated.	.853***	.949	.932	.787	Yes
	I was intrigued by a new idea.	.903***				
	I unexpectedly and spontaneously got new ideas.	.903***				
	My horizon was broadened.	.896***				
	I discovered something new.	.879***				
LOC2: Inspired-to	I was inspired to buy something.	.963***	.984	.980	.926	Yes
	I felt a desire to buy something.	.953***				
	My interest to buy something was increased.	.979***				
	I was motivated to buy something.	.954***				
	I felt an urge to buy something.	.963***				

Note: * p < .1; ** p < .05; *** p < .01; [1] Composite Reliability; [2] Discriminant Validity

Table 3.7 HOC—Reflective measurement assessment of CI by Böttger et al. (2017)

Indicator	Loading	C.R.[1]	Cronbach's α	AVE	D.V.[2]
Inspired-by	.921***	.916	.816	.844	Yes
Inspired-to	.917***				

Note: * p < .1; ** p < .05; *** p < .01; [1] Composite Reliability; [2] Discriminant Validity

Assessment of the Reflective Measures

Our structural model included seven reflectively-measured constructs: two endogenous variables, willingness to pay and purchase intention; one moderator variable, involvement; one exogenous variable, brand attitude; and two control variables, ad liking and brand familiarity. We checked for internal consistency, individual reliability, and convergent validity within the reflective measurements by assessing the composite reliability, Cronbach's alpha values, loading levels and AVE of all multi-item measures. In order to assess discriminant validity, we first examined the Fornell-Larcker criterion. All square roots of the AVE of the diagonals should be higher than the latent variable correlations of the non-diagonals (Fornell & Larcker, 1981), which was the case in our model. Next, we checked all cross-loadings and whether the indicators of each construct loaded highest on their associated construct, which was the case for all indicators. The HTMT$_{reference}$ assessment supported this finding with all values below the threshold of 1.0. All constructs were therefore discriminant valid. Table 3.8 summarizes the evaluation criteria.[3] The results showed overall good values, which indicated reliability and validity of the reflective measures.

Table 3.8   Reflective measurement assessment

Construct	Item	Loading	C.R.[1]	Cron-bach's α	AVE	D.V.[2]
Willingness to Pay	Are you willing to pay more for Nike than for other brands in the same product category?	.995***	.995	.990	.990	Yes
	Are you willing to pay a higher price for Nike than for other brands?	.995***				
Purchase Intention	For my next purchase of sports equipment, I intend to buy a Nike brand.	.970***	.971	.939	.943	Yes
	How likely is it that you would buy this brand (Nike)?	.972***				
Involvement	Indicate how well one or the other adjective in each pair describes what the brand Nike is for you:		.941	.926	.763	Yes

(continued)

---

[3] For the single-item measures of ad liking and brand familiarity, the internal consistency reliability cannot be estimated (Wanous & Reichers, 1996).

Table 3.8 (continued)

Construct	Item	Loading	C.R.[1]	Cron-bach's α	AVE	D.V.[2]
	➔ mportant-Unimportant	.889***				
	➔ Interesting-Boring	.859***				
	➔ Relevant-Irrelevant	.877***				
	➔ Meaningful-Not Meaningful	.920***				
	➔ Useful-Useless	.818***				
Brand Attitude	Indicate how well one or the other adjective in each pair describes your overall feeling of Nike:		.937	.897	.823	Yes
	➔ Bad-Good	.968***				
	➔ Pleasant-Unpleasant[3]	.812***				
	➔ Dislike-Like	.949***				

Note: * p < .1; ** p < .05; *** p < .01; [1] Composite Reliability; [2] Discriminant Validity; [3] reversely coded

As the only formatively-measured constructs have been already checked within the assessment of the HOC, we proceeded directly with the evaluation of the structural model.

Assessment of the Structural Model
First, multicollinearity among the independent variables was assessed by means of the VIF. The results did not raise any concern as all values were below the critical threshold of 5 ($VIF_{Min} = 1.071$; $VIF_{Max} = 4.357$). In order to assess the path coefficients, we split the model into three separate ones, namely one customer inspiration model (CI), one model including customer inspiration and brand attitude (CI-BA), and one model including both customer inspiration constructs (CI-CB).

Table 3.9 shows the results of the CI model. Customer inspiration had a significant positive relationship with purchase intention, even after controlling for involvement, brand familiarity, ad liking, income, gender, and age (PC = .676***). The same applied for the relationship on willingness to pay (PC = .668***). Within the CI-BA model (Table 3.10), customer inspiration showed significant positive relationships with purchase intention (PC = .536***) and willingness to pay (PC = .611***). Brand attitude had a significant positive relationship with purchase intention (PC = .231**). The relationship between brand attitude and willingness to pay was not significant (PC = .094). The control conditions remained the same. Table 3.11 shows the results of the CI-CB model. The relationship with customer inspiration and purchase intention (PC = .564***) and willingness to pay (PC = .570***) was positive and significant. The same applied for customer inspiration by Böttger et al. (2017) with purchase intention (PC = .209**) and willingness to pay (PC = .181**).

We assessed the model quality in terms of its in-sample (explanatory power) and out-of-sample predictive quality (predictive power) as well as the effect size of each predictor variable. We applied the same logic and calculated the values for all three models. The R^2 value is a measure of the predictive accuracy of the model. We further assessed the adjusted R^2 value, which takes the complexity of the model into account. In the CI model, customer inspiration explained a moderate amount of the variance of purchase intention and willingness to pay (.693/.652). For the CI-BA model, we assessed the adjusted R^2 value, as we had two exogenous variables pointing to the endogenous variables. With values of .710 and .652 for purchase intention and willingness to pay, respectively, the CI-BA model showed a slightly higher explanatory power for purchase intention and a similar explanatory power for willingness to pay as in the CI model. Within the CI-CB model, adjusted R^2 values of .706 for purchase intention and .661 for willingness to pay indicated that the CI-CB model explained the highest amount of willingness to pay, but slightly less of purchase intention than the CI-BA model. The effect size (f^2) for each predictor variable indicates the change in R^2 value when the respective variable is excluded from the structural model (Hair et al., 2014). In Tables 3.10 and 3.11, the effect sizes of each predictor variable are provided. The effect size of customer inspiration on purchase intention was large in both models (.320/.370) compared with brand attitude (.068) and customer inspiration by Böttger et al. (2017) (.054) (J. Cohen, 1988). The same applied for willingness to pay, where customer inspiration showed large effect sizes (.346/.328) compared with the other two predictor variables (f^2_{BA} = .009; f^2_{CB} = .035). For assessing the predictive relevance of the structural model, we used the Stone-Geisser's Q^2 value with an omission distance of seven. The results (Table 3.12) suggested that all three models had a strong predictive power for purchase intention and willingness to pay with values above .500.

Table 3.9 Structural model assessment—CI model

Variable	Purchase Intention		Willingness to Pay	
	Path Coefficients	Effect Size (f^2)	Path Coefficients	Effect Size (f^2)
Customer Inspiration	.676***	.696	.668***	.599
Control				
Involvement	.088 (NS)	.025	.094*	.025
Brand Familiarity	.068 (NS)	.014	.079 (NS)	.017
Ad Liking	.170*	.053	.136*	.030
Income	.026 (NS)	.002	.022 (NS)	.001
Gender	.013 (NS)	.000	.022 (NS)	.001
Age	−.028 (NS)	.002	−.016 (NS)	.001

Note: * p < .1; ** p < .05; *** p < .01; NS = not significant

Table 3.10 Structural model assessment—CI-BA model

Variable	Purchase Intention		Willingness to Pay	
	Path Coefficients	Effect Size (f^2)	Path Coefficients	Effect Size (f^2)
Customer Inspiration	.536***	.320	.611***	.346
Brand Attitude	.231**	.068	.094 (NS)	.009
Control				
Involvement	.090*	.028	.095*	.026
Brand Familiarity	.041 (NS)	.005	.068 (NS)	.012
Ad Liking	.116 (NS)	.024	.114 (NS)	.019
Income	.042 (NS)	.006	.028 (NS)	.002
Gender	.019 (NS)	.001	−.020 (NS)	.001
Age	−.053 (NS)	.009	−.027 (NS)	.002

Note: * p < .1; ** p < .05; *** p < .01; NS = not significant

Comparing Explanatory Power

In addition to the structural model assessment, we wanted to examine whether the changes in R^2 dependent on each predictor variable were significant. We exported the LVSs of the CI-BA and CI-CB models from SmartPLS into SPSS and calculated stepwise multiple linear regression models. First, we compared

Table 3.11 Structural model assessment—CI-CB model

Variable	Purchase Intention		Willingness to Pay	
	Path Coefficients	Effect Size (f^2)	Path Coefficients	Effect Size (f^2)
Customer Inspiration	.564***	.370	.570***	.328
Customer Inspiration (Böttger et al., 2017)	.209**	.054	.181**	.035
Control				
Involvement	.097*	.031	.102*	.030
Brand Familiarity	.054 (NS)	.009	.067 (NS)	.012
Ad Liking	.098 (NS)	.016	.073 (NS)	.008
Income	.030 (NS)	.003	.025 (NS)	.002
Gender	−.005 (NS)	.000	−.038 (NS)	.004
Age	−.020 (NS)	.001	−.010 (NS)	.000

Note: * $p < .1$; ** $p < .05$; *** $p < .01$; NS = not significant

Table 3.12 Explanatory and predictive power

Predictor Variable(s) in Model	Dependent Variable	Explanatory Power (R^2/ Adj. R^2)	Predictive Power (Q^2)
Customer Inspiration →	Purchase Intention	.713 / .693	.642
	Willingness to pay	.675 / .652	.649
Customer Inspiration → Brand Attitude →	Purchase Intention	.731 / .710	.662
	Willingness to pay	.678 / .652	.651
Customer Inspiration → Customer Inspiration (Böttger et al., 2017) →	Purchase Intention	.727 / .706	.654
	Willingness to pay	.686 / .661	.661

the predictive power of customer inspiration and brand attitude. The results for the prediction of purchase intention are shown in Table 3.13. The ΔR^2 between models 1.1 and 1.2 showed a significant change of .024 after adding brand attitude into the model. By comparison, the ΔR^2 between models 2.1 and 2.2 was also significant but higher with a value of .161 after adding customer inspiration into the model. These results indicated that the relative predictive power of customer inspiration on purchase intention was higher than for brand attitude.

We obtained similar results for the prediction of willingness to pay a price premium (Table 3.14). The relative predictive power of customer inspiration was even higher compared with brand attitude in this model, indicated by an insignificant ΔR^2 between the model 1.1 and 1.2 of .007. The ΔR^2 between models 2.1 and 2.2 showed a high value of .200 and was significant.

Table 3.13 Stepwise multiple linear regression results for PI

Model: Predictors for PI	R^2	Adj. R^2	ΔR^2	p-Value (ΔR^2)
1.1: CI	.684	.681	.684	.000***
1.2: CI, BA	.708	.703	.024	.003***
2.1: BA	.547	.543	.547	.000***
2.2: BA, CI	.708	.703	.161	.000***
3: CI, BA, BF	.711	.703	.003	.304 (NS)
4: CI, BA, BF, Iv	.719	.708	.008	.086*
5: CI, BA, BF, Iv, In	.720	.707	.001	.483 (NS)
6: CI, BA, BF, Iv, In, G	.722	.706	.001	.477 (NS)
7: CI, BA, BF, Iv, In, G, A	.725	.706	.003	.309 (NS)

Note: * p < .1; ** p < .05; *** p < .01; NS = not significant;
PI = Purchase Intention; CI = Customer Inspiration; BA = Brand Attitude; BF = Brand Familiarity; Iv = Involvement; In = Income; G = Gender; A = Age

Table 3.14 Stepwise multiple linear regression results for WP

Model: Predictors for WP	R^2	Adj. R^2	ΔR^2	p-Value (ΔR^2)
1.1: CI	.650	.647	.650	.000***
1.2: CI, BA	.657	.650	.007	.153 (NS)
2.1: BA	.457	.452	.457	.000***
2.2: BA, CI	.657	.650	.200	.000***
3: CI, BA, BF	.662	.652	.005	.198 (NS)
4: CI, BA, BF, Iv	.670	.658	.008	.111 (NS)
5: CI, BA, BF, Iv, In	.671	.655	.001	.672 (NS)
6: CI, BA, BF, Iv, In, G	.671	.652	.000	.899 (NS)
7: CI, BA, BF, Iv, In, G, A	.672	.649	.001	.612 (NS)

Note: * p < .1; ** p < .05; *** p < .01; NS = not significant;
WP = Willingness to Pay a Price Premium; CI = Customer Inspiration; BA = Brand Attitude; BF = Brand Familiarity; Iv = Involvement; In = Income; G = Gender; A = Age

Next, we compared the predictive relevance of the two customer inspiration constructs. For the prediction of purchase intention, both constructs added significant values of ΔR^2 into the model (Table 3.15). With a value of .168 of customer inspiration, the absolute amount of the ΔR^2 value was higher than for customer inspiration by Böttger et al. (2017), with a value of .025. A similar result was obtained for willingness to pay, as shown in Table 3.16. With a value of .017, the ΔR^2 value dependent of customer inspiration by Böttger et al. (2017) is lower than for customer inspiration (.176). These results indicate that the newly-developed construct of customer inspiration has a higher explanatory power than the established measure.

Table 3.15 Stepwise multiple linear regression results for PI

Model: Predictors for PI	R^2	Adj. R^2	ΔR^2	p-Value (ΔR^2)
1.1: CI	.684	.681	.684	.000***
1.2: CI, CB	.709	.704	.025	.003***
2.1: CB	.541	.537	.541	.000***
2.2: CB, CI	.709	.704	.168	.000***
3: CI, CB, BF	.713	.705	.004	.226 (NS)
4: CI, CB, BF, Iv	.722	.712	.009	.066*
5: CI, CB, BF, Iv, In	.723	.710	.001	.610 (NS)
6: CI, CB, BF, Iv, In, G	.723	.707	.000	.979 (NS)
7: CI, CB, BF, Iv, In, G, A	.723	.704	.000	.734 (NS)

Note: * $p < .1$; ** $p < .05$; *** $p < .01$; NS = not significant;
PI = Purchase Intention; CI = Customer Inspiration; CB = Customer Inspiration (Böttger et al., 2017); BF = Brand Familiarity; Iv = Involvement; In = Income; G = Gender; A = Age

Moderation Analysis
For the analysis concerning whether involvement served as a moderator for the relationship between customer inspiration and willingness to pay a price premium (Table 3.17), we used the two-stage calculation method with a standardized interaction term (Becker, Ringle, & Sarstedt, 2018). Although a significant path coefficient of involvement on willingness to pay was found (PC = .094*), the interaction term was not significant. Hence, involvement did not moderate the effect of customer inspiration on willingness to pay. We also tested whether ad liking might moderate the effect of customer inspiration on willingness to pay and purchase intention, since the model showed a significant effect of ad liking on both variables. A moderation analysis revealed a significant interaction term of ad liking and customer inspiration on willingness to pay. This was not the case for the effect on purchase intention.

Table 3.16 Stepwise multiple linear regression results for WP

Model: Predictors for WP	R^2	Adj. R^2	ΔR^2	p-Value (ΔR^2)
1.1: CI	.650	.647	.650	.000***
1.2: CI, CB	.667	.660	.017	.023**
2.1: CB	.490	.486	.490	.000***
2.2: CB, CI	.667	.660	.176	.000***
3: CI, CB, BF	.672	.663	.005	.186 (NS)
4: CI, CB, BF, Iv	.682	.670	.009	.080*
5: CI, CB, BF, Iv, In	.682	.667	.000	.701 (NS)
6: CI, CB, BF, Iv, In, G	.683	.665	.001	.537 (NS)
7: CI, CB, BF, Iv, In, G, A	.683	.662	.000	.877 (NS)

Note: * p < .1; ** p < .05; *** p < .01; NS = not significant;
WP = Willingness to Pay a Price Premium; CI = Customer Inspiration; CB = Customer Inspiration (Böttger et al., 2017);
BF = Brand Familiarity; Iv = Involvement; In = Income; G = Gender; A = Age

Table 3.17 Results of moderation analysis

Moderator Variable	Independent Variable	Dependent Variable	Effect Size (f^2) of Moderator	Path Coefficient
Ad Liking	Customer Inspiration	Purchase Intention	.004	.043 (NS)
	Customer Inspiration	Willingness to pay	.075	.183***
Involvement	Customer Inspiration	Willingness to pay	.005	.038 (NS)

Note: * p < .1; ** p < .05; *** p < .01; NS = not significant

Additional Calculations

We further assessed whether brand attitude strength—operationalized as attitude valence x attitude certainty—reveals different results. Based on Fazio (1990) and Krosnick et al. (1993), the strength of a brand evaluation predicts behavior. Accordingly, we multiplied each valence item with the attitude certainty as in Park et al. (2010) to measure attitude strength and estimated the structural model according to the previously-described procedure. The results displayed in Table 3.18 show that attitude strength did not change the explanatory power of the brand attitude constructs. The path coefficient of each purchase intention even turned non-significant (PC = .085).

Table 3.18 Structural model assessment with brand attitude strength

Variable	Purchase Intention		Willingness to Pay	
	Path Coefficients	Effect Size (f^2)	Path Coefficients	Effect Size (f^2)
Customer Inspiration	.626***	.435	.657***	.419
Brand Attitude Strength	.085 (NS)	.010	.018 (NS)	.000
R^2 I Adj. R^2 I Q^2	.716 I .693 I .647		.675 I .649 I .650	
Control				
Involvement	.082 (NS)	.022	.093*	.024
Brand Familiarity	.052 (NS)	.008	.076 (NS)	.014
Ad Liking	.158*	.045	.133*	.028
Income	.029 (NS)	.003	.022 (NS)	.001
Gender	.016 (NS)	.001	−.022 (NS)	.001
Age	−.043 (NS)	.005	−.020 (NS)	.001

Note: * $p < .1$; ** $p < .05$; *** $p < .01$; NS = not significant

Summary of Results

In the previous section, we ran several analyses to test our hypothesis. We started with the assessment of higher-order structures of the two customer inspiration constructs. The analysis results were in favor of the internal consistency, convergent validity, and discriminant validity of the LOCs of both constructs. For the HOC of customer inspiration, our assessment confirmed convergent validity as well as significant outer loadings. For the HOC of customer inspiration by Böttger et al. (2017), our assessment confirmed internal consistency, convergent validity and discriminant validity. We then assessed the reflective measures as well as the structural model, which led us to the examination of our hypothesis. In H_{1a} and H_{1b}, we hypothesized that consumers who have a higher level of customer inspiration show a higher level of purchase intention and willingness to pay a price premium. The model indicated that customer inspiration is a good predictor of purchase intention (PC = .676***; $f^2 = .696$; $R^2 = .713$) and willingness to pay (PC = .668***; $f^2 = .599$; $R^2 = .675$) while controlling for ad liking, brand familiarity, income, gender, and age. Accordingly, the results are in support of H_{1a} and H_{1b}.

The hypothesized moderating effect of involvement (H_{2a} and H_{2b}) was not supported in our model. One potential reason could be low variance among the involvement indicators ($M_{min} = 4.62$; $M_{max} = 5.59$; $SD_{min} = 1.32$; $SD_{max} = 1.59$), which reflect a homogenous involvement level towards the product. We will assess a potential moderating effect of involvement again in study 2. We additionally examined whether ad liking moderates the effect of customer inspiration on willingness to pay and purchase intention. We found a significant interaction effect for willingness to pay.

In H_{3a}, we hypothesized that customer inspiration is a better predictor for the willingness to pay a price premium than brand attitude. In order to test H_{3a}, we assessed adjusted R^2 values of willingness to pay of all models, as well as the f^2 effect sizes of both predictor variables. The CI-BA model showed an adjusted R^2 value of .652 compared with .652 for the CI model. Hence, the CI model indicated the same predictive accuracy as the CI-BA model. The effect size of customer inspiration was large (.320) compared with brand attitude (.068) within the CI-BA model. An additional assessment of the ΔR^2 revealed that customer inspiration added a significant ΔR^2 of .200 after including it as the predictor into the model. By comparison, the ΔR^2 of brand attitude was .007 and insignificant. Therefore, these results are in support of H_{3a}. We applied the same approach to test H_{3b}. The CI-BA model had the highest predictive accuracy for purchase intention, with an adjusted R^2 of .710. The ΔR^2 of customer inspiration was .161 and significant. The ΔR^2 of brand attitude was also significant but lower with a value of .024. These results are in favor of H_{3b}, confirming that customer inspiration is a better predictor of purchase intention than brand attitude. A recalculation of the model using brand attitude strength as a predictor variable did not add any new information.

In addition, we compared the two customer inspiration constructs in terms of their explanatory power to test H_{4a} and H_{4b}. We estimated an additional structural model that contained both constructs as predictor variables and applied the same method as before when testing H_{3a} and H_{3b}. For the prediction of willingness to pay (H_{4a}), the CI-CB model indicated a higher adjusted R^2 value of .661 compared with .652 for the CI model. The effect size of customer inspiration was higher than of customer inspiration by Böttger et al. (2017) with a value of .328 compared with .035. The stepwise multiple regression model showed significant ΔR^2 values of both predictor variables. However, the absolute amount of our customer inspiration construct was higher with a value of .176 compared with .017 for the established customer inspiration construct. For testing H_{4b}, we applied the same logic and compared adjusted R^2 values of the CI model (.693) and the CI-CB model (.706), as well as effect sizes and ΔR^2 values. For the explanation of purchase intention, the newly-developed construct customer inspiration ($f^2 = .270$; $\Delta R^2 = .168^{***}$) showed better results than the established construct ($f^2 = .054$; $\Delta R^2 = .025^{***}$). These results are in support of H_{4b}. Table 3.19 summarizes all results of the hypotheses.

Table 3.19 Overview of the hypotheses results

H_{1a}	Customers who show a higher level of customer inspiration towards a brand have a higher willingness to pay a price premium for the brand.	**Supported**
H_{1b}	Customers who show a higher level of customer inspiration towards a brand have higher purchase intention for the brand.	**Supported**
H_{2a}	Involvement with the product moderates the effect of customer inspiration on the willingness to pay a price premium in the sense that the more involved that a customer is with the product, the higher the willingness to pay a price premium.	Not Supported
H_{2b}	Involvement with the product moderates the effect of customer inspiration on purchase intention in the sense that the more involved that a customer is with the product, the higher the purchase intention.	Not Supported
H_{3a}	Customer inspiration is a better predictor of a consumer's willingness to pay a price premium than brand attitude.	**Supported**
H_{3b}	Customer inspiration is a better predictor of a consumer's purchase intention than brand attitude.	**Supported**
H_{4a}	Customer inspiration is a better predictor of a consumer's willingness to pay a price premium than customer inspiration by Böttger et al. (2017).	**Supported**
H_{4b}	Customer inspiration is a better predictor of a consumer's purchase intention than customer inspiration by Böttger et al. (2017).	**Supported**

3.4 Study 2

3.4.1 Survey Design and Measures

As study 1 included the evaluation of the brand Nike, we wanted to conduct a second study to test whether the results can be replicated with another brand from a different industry. In addition, we wanted to test whether we can find support for H_{2a} and H_{2b} under these conditions. Therefore, we replicated study 1 and conducted a second online survey with the market research software Qualtrics. Again, convenience sampling was applied as we recruited survey respondents on Mturk with the help of the intermediary service provider, CloudResearch. The study design and the measures remained identical, apart from the brand that participants had to evaluate. We chose Tesla—the electric car company—for two reasons (Tesla, 2020): first, Tesla was one of the top five inspiring brands from our pre-study of **Study II**; and second, as Tesla has been in the news with mixed valence quite often (Rapier, 2019), we expected that most of the participants know the brand at least by name and have a certain attitude towards the brand.

3.4.2 Analysis and Results

Descriptive Statistics
Among the 144 completed surveys, we eliminated those respondents who showed zero variance in their brand assessments of the focal constructs, whereby 123 survey remained after this step. 36.6% of the participants were female, 62.6% male and 0.8% diverse. Participants were between 19 and 76 years old (M: 40.17, SD: 12.24) and they were all located in the United States. Descriptive statistics are provided in Appendix 2 within the Electronic Supplementary Material.

Assessment of the Higher-Order Construct
For data analysis purposes, we again used the SmartPLS software (Ringle et al., 2015) and started with the assessment of the HOC of customer inspiration. Composite reliability, Cronbach's alpha values, loadings levels, and the AVE assessed internal consistency, indicator reliability and convergent validity of the reflective measurements for the three LOCs. For the assessment of discriminant validity, we chose the heterotrait-monotrait ratio of correlations (HTMT) (Henseler, Ringle, & Sarstedt, 2014). The HTMT$_{reference}$ value was again below the threshold of 1.0, which is an indicator of discriminant validity. Since the results (Appendix 3 within the Electronic Supplementary Material) showed satisfactory quality of the measurement of the LOCs, we proceeded with the assessment of the formative measures of customer inspiration between the three LOCs with the HOC as the second stage of the hierarchical component model assessment.

The LOCs were again replaced by the LVSs, which served as manifest indicators for customer inspiration. The VIF evaluates the structure of the formative measures to uncover potential collinearity issues (Hair et al., 2014). Two of the VIFs were below 5 (3.205/3.835). Activation had a VIF of 5.339. Since this value is still close to the threshold, we did not raise any collinearity issues. Next, outer weights and outer loadings of the HOC were assessed. Outer weights represent the indicators' relative contribution to the overall construct and the outer loadings the absolute contribution. The outer weights of transformation and activation—which were both non-significant and negative in the case of transformation—indicated that the relative importance of the transformation and activation component was low compared with connection. As the outer loadings of all three components were high and significant with values above .500, the outer weights can be interpreted as absolutely but not relatively important. As the construct is based on expert knowledge and conceptualized based on both managerial and consumer perspective (**Study II**), we kept the non-significant indicators as proposed by Hair et al. (2014). Table 3.20 summarizes the HOC results.

Table 3.20 HOC—Formative measurement assessment

Indicator	VIF	Outer Weights	Outer Loadings
Connection	3.205	1.098***	.991***
Transformation	3.835	−.242 (NS)	.655***
Activation	5.339	.089 (NS)	.798***

Note: * p < .1; ** p < .05; *** p < .01

For inspecting criterion validity, we connected customer inspiration with the criterion variable of purchase intention. The R^2 value showed a moderate value of .502. The Stone-Geisser's Q^2 value of the construct was .455, indicating a moderate level of predictive relevance for the criterion variable. Overall, the results were in favor of the validity of the customer inspiration construct. We next assessed the HOC of customer inspiration by Böttger et al. (2017). The results of the LOC assessment are shown in Appendix 4 within the Electronic Supplementary Material, delivering good results. The subsequent HOC assessment is presented in Table 3.21. The results are indicative of internal consistency, individual reliability, and convergent validity as well as discriminant validity of the HOC.

Table 3.21 HOC—Reflective measurement assessment of CI by Böttger et al. (2017)

Indicator	Loading	C.R.[1]	Cronbach's α	AVE	D.V.[2]
Inspired-by	.902***	.916	.819	.845	Yes
Inspired-to	.936***				

Note: * p < .1; ** p < .05; *** p < .01; [1] Composite Reliability; [2] Discriminant Validity

Assessment of the Reflective Measures
We proceeded with the assessment of the reflective measures of the model (Table 3.22). We analyzed internal consistency, individual reliability, and convergent validity within the reflective measurements of the model by appraising composite reliability, Cronbach's alpha values, loading levels and AVE. The maximum

HTMT value was again below the threshold of .900 (.569), which is an indicator of discriminant validity. As all values showed good results and were in favor of reliability and validity of all reflective measures, we proceeded with the assessment of the structural model.

Table 3.22 Reflective measurement assessment

Construct	Item	Loading	C.R.[1]	Cronbach's α	AVE	D.V.[2]
Willingness to Pay	Are you willing to pay more for this brand than for other brands in the same product category?	.991***	.991	.982	.982	Yes
	Are you willing to pay a higher price for this brand than for other brands?	.991***				
Purchase Intention	For my next purchase of a car, I intend to buy one from Tesla.	.972***	.971	.941	.944	Yes
	How likely is it that you would buy the presented car in the ad?	.972***				
Involvement	For you, cars such as advertised in the ad are ...		.937	.915	.748	Yes
	→ Important-Unimportant	.856***				
	→ Interesting-Boring	.765***				
	→ Relevant-Irrelevant	.917***				
	→ Meaningful-Not Meaningful	.911***				
	→ Useful-Useless	.867***				
Brand Attitude	Indicate how well one or the other adjective in each pair describes your overall feeling of the brand Tesla.		.903	.842	.761	Yes
	→ Bad-Good	.954***				
	→ Pleasant-Unpleasant[3]	.677***				
	→ Dislike-Like	.957***				

Note: * p < .1 ; ** p < .05 *** p < .01;[1] Composite Reliability; [2] Discriminant validity: [3] reversely coded

Assessment of the Structural Model

We started by assessing collinearity among all independent variables. Since the VIF values that ranged between 1.098 and 3.211 were all below the critical threshold of 5, multicollinearity was not an issue among the independent variables (Hair et al., 2014). In order to assess the structural models, we followed the logic of study 1 and built three separate models. The results of the path coefficients and effect sizes of each model are assembled in Tables 3.23–3.25.

Within the CI model (Table 3.23), we found a significant path coefficient for customer inspiration on purchase intention (PC = .595***) and willingness to pay (PC = .404***) while controlling for involvement, brand familiarity, ad liking, income, gender, and age. Within the CI-BA model (Table 3.24), we found a significant path coefficient of brand attitude on willingness to pay (PC = .291***). No significant effect of brand attitude on purchase intention could be found. The path coefficients of customer inspiration were again positive and significant (PC$_{PI}$ = .557***; PC$_{WP}$ = .276***). Within the CI-CB model (Table 3.25), we found a significant path coefficient between customer inspiration and purchase intention (PC = .521***) as well as willingness to pay (PC = .385***). Customer inspiration by Böttger et al. (2017) showed no significant effect on purchase intention (PC = .126), nor willingness to pay (PC = .031).

Table 3.23 Structural model assessment—CI model

Variable	Purchase Intention		Willingness to Pay	
	Path Coefficients	Effect Size (f^2)	Path Coefficients	Effect Size (f^2)
Customer Inspiration	.595***	.445	.404***	.162
Control				
Involvement	.123 (NS)	.021	.241**	.063
Brand Familiarity	.108 (NS)	.021	.046 (NS)	.003
Ad Liking	.009 (NS)	.000	−.061 (NS)	.005
Income	−.077 (NS)	.012	−.009 (NS)	.000
Gender	−.059 (NS)	.007	−.110 (NS)	.020
Age	−.133**	.033	−.266***	.106

Note: * p < .1; ** p < .05; *** p < .01; NS = not significant

Table 3.24 Structural model assessment—CI-BA model

Variable	Purchase Intention		Willingness to Pay	
	Path Coefficients	Effect Size (f^2)	Path Coefficients	Effect Size (f^2)
Customer Inspiration	.557***	.320	.276***	.067
Brand Attitude	.085 (NS)	.008	.291***	.076
Control				
Involvement	.114 (NS)	.017	.209**	.050
Brand Familiarity	.105 (NS)	.020	.036 (NS)	.002
Ad Liking	−.019 (NS)	.001	−.155**	.031
Income	−.080 (NS)	.014	−.020 (NS)	.001
Gender	−.052 (NS)	.006	−.087 (NS)	.014
Age	−.132**	.033	−.265***	.113

Note: * $p < .1$; ** $p < .05$; *** $p < .01$; NS = not significant

Table 3.25 Structural model assessment—CI-CB model

Variable	Purchase Intention		Willingness to Pay	
	Path Coefficients	Effect Size (f^2)	Path Coefficients	Effect Size (f^2)
Customer Inspiration	.521***	.232	.385***	.099
Customer Inspiration (Böttger et al., 2017)	.126 (NS)	.014	.031 (NS)	.001
Control				
Involvement	.095 (NS)	.011	.234**	.055
Brand Familiarity	.111 (NS)	.022	.047 (NS)	.003
Ad Liking	.004 (NS)	.000	−.062 (NS)	.005
Income	−.085 (NS)	.015	−.011 (NS)	.000
Gender	−.040 (NS)	.003	−.105 (NS)	.018
Age	−.117*	.026	−.262***	.100

Note: * $p < .1$; ** $p < .05$; *** $p < .01$; NS = not significant

We also estimated R^2, adjusted R^2 and Q^2 values for each of the models (Table 3.26). The adjusted R^2 values within the CI model were moderate for willingness to pay (.413) and purchase intention (.535). The CI-BA model had the same adjusted R^2 value for purchase intention (.535) and a slightly higher value for willingness to pay (.450). The CI-CB model showed an adjusted R^2 value of .538 for purchase intention and .408 for willingness to pay. Hence, the CI-CB model yielded he highest adjusted R^2 value for the explanation of purchase intention and the lowest adjusted R^2 value for willingness to pay compared with the other two models. The effect sizes of customer inspiration in the CI-BA model were large for purchase intention (.320) and medium for willingness to pay (.067). Brand attitude showed a small effect size on purchase intention (.008) and a medium effect size on willingness to pay (.076) (J. Cohen, 1988). Within the CI-CB model, effect sizes of customer inspiration are medium for purchase intention (.232) and willingness to pay (.099) compared with customer inspiration by Böttger et al. (2017), which showed small values (.014/.001). The Stone-Geisser's Q values with an omission distance of seven indicated that the predictive relevance of the CI-BA model was highest for willingness to pay (.435). The CI-CB model had the highest predictive relevance for purchase intention (.505).

Table 3.26 Explanatory and predictive power

Predictor Variable(s) in Model	Dependent Variable	Explanatory Power (R^2/ Adj. R^2)	Predictive Power (Q^2)
Customer Inspiration ➜	Purchase Intention	.562 / .535	.498
	Willingness to pay	.447 / .413	.396
Customer Inspiration ➜ Brand Attitude ➜	Purchase Intention	.565 / .535	.501
	Willingness to pay	.486 / .450	.435
Customer Inspiration ➜ Customer Inspiration (Böttger et al., 2017) ➜	Purchase Intention	.568 / .538	.505
	Willingness to pay	.447 / .408	.388

Comparing Explanatory Power
In order to gage whether the changes in R^2 values were significant, we again calculated ΔR^2 values by means of stepwise multiple linear regression models in SPSS. We started with the comparison of customer inspiration and brand attitude. The results for purchase intention are presented in Table 3.27. The ΔR^2 assigned to customer inspiration had a value of .231 and was significant. Brand attitude did not add any significant change in R^2 to the model. For the explanation of

willingness to pay (Table 3.28), both predictor variables added significant ΔR^2 to the model. With a value of .084, the change assigned to customer inspiration was higher than for brand attitude (.043).

Table 3.27 Stepwise multiple linear regression results for PI

Model: Predictors for PI	R^2	Adj. R^2	ΔR^2	p-Value (ΔR^2)
1.1: BA	.275	.269	.275	.000***
1.2: BA, CI	.506	.498	.231	.000***
2.1: CI	.499	.495	.499	.000***
2.2: CI, BA	.506	.498	.007	.198 (NS)
3: BA, CI, BF	.527	.515	.021	.025**
4: BA, CI, BF, AL	.527	.511	.000	.934 (NS)
5: BA, CI, BF, AL, Iv	.539	.520	.012	.078*
6: BA, CI, BF, AL, Iv, In	.549	.526	.010	.109 (NS)
7: BA, CI, BF, AL, Iv, In, G	.551	.523	.001	.555 (NS)
8: BA, CI, BF, AL, Iv, In, G, A	.565	.535	.014	.054*

Note: * $p < .1$; ** $p < .05$; *** $p < .01$; NS = not significant;
PI = Purchase Intention; BA = Brand Attitude; CI = Customer Inspiration; BF = Brand Familiarity; AL = Ad Liking; Iv = Involvement; In = Income; G = Gender; A = Age

Table 3.28 Stepwise multiple linear regression results for WP

Model: Predictors for WP	R^2	Adj. R^2	ΔR^2	p-Value (ΔR^2)
1.1: BA	.274	.268	.274	.000***
1.2: BA, CI	.358	.347	.084	.000***
2.1: CI	.315	.309	.315	.000***
2.2: CI, BA	.358	.347	.043	.006***
3: BA, CI, BF	.373	.357	.015	.091*
4: BA, CI, BF, AL	.383	.362	.010	.167 (NS)
5: BA, CI, BF, AL, Iv	.420	.395	.037	.007***
6: BA, CI, BF, AL, Iv, In	.424	.395	.004	.361 (NS)
7: BA, CI, BF, AL, Iv, In, G	.428	.393	.003	.420 (NS)
8: BA, CI, BF, AL, Iv, In, G, A	.486	.450	.058	.000***

Note: * $p < .1$; ** $p < .05$; *** $p < .01$; NS = not significant;
WP = Willingness to Pay a Price Premium; BA = Brand Attitude; CI = Customer Inspiration; BF = Brand Familiarity; AL = Ad Liking; Iv = Involvement; In = Income; G = Gender; A = Age

We proceeded with the comparison of the two customer inspiration constructs. Table 3.29 shows the results for the explanation of purchase intention. With a value of .143, the ΔR^2 assigned to customer inspiration is higher compared with customer inspiration by Böttger et al. (2017) ($\Delta R^2 = .017$). The same applies for the explanation of willingness to pay (Table 3.30). With a value of .079, the ΔR^2 assigned to customer inspiration is higher than the value of .016 assigned to customer inspiration by Böttger et al. (2017). This analysis shows that the construct of customer inspiration has the highest explanatory power compared with brand attitude and customer inspiration conceptualized by Böttger et al. (2017).

Table 3.29 Stepwise multiple linear regression results for PI

Model: Predictors for PI	R^2	Adj. R^2	ΔR^2	p-Value (ΔR^2)
1.1: CI	.499	.495	.499	.000***
1.2: CI, CB	.516	.508	.017	.045**
2.1: CB	.373	.368	.373	.000***
2.2: CB, CI	.516	.508	.143	.000***
3: CI, CB, BF	.537	.525	.021	.022**
4: CI, CB, BF, AL	.538	.522	.001	.708 (NS)
5: CI, CB, BF, AL, Iv	.545	.526	.008	.159 (NS)
6: CI, CB, BF, AL, Iv, In	.556	.534	.011	.093*
7: CI, CB, BF, AL, Iv, In, G	.557	.530	.000	.725 (NS)
8: CI, CB, BF, AL, Iv, In, G, A	.568	.538	.011	.090*

Note: * p < .1; ** p < .05; *** p < .01; NS = not significant;
PI = Purchase Intention; CI = Customer Inspiration; CB = Customer Inspiration by Böttger et al. (2017); BF = Brand Familiarity; AL = Ad Liking; Iv = Involvement; In = Income; G = Gender; A = Age

Assessment of Moderation Effects
As a final step, we wanted to check potential moderation effects with a two-staged mean standardized approach (Becker et al., 2018). As involvement only showed a significant path coefficient on willingness to pay within the CI model, we assessed whether the interaction term of customer inspiration and involvement had a significant effect on the dependent variable. The results showed no effect, meaning that involvement did not moderate the effect. For exploration reasons, we also assessed a potential moderating effect of age on the predictive relevance of customer inspiration. The analysis revealed no significant interaction term (Table 3.31). Hence, no moderation effect was found.

Table 3.30 Stepwise multiple linear regression results for WP

Model: Predictors for WP	R^2	**Adj. R^2**	**ΔR^2**	**p-Value (ΔR^2)**
1.1: CI	.315	.309	.315	.000***
1.2: CI, CB	.331	.320	.016	.090*
2.1: CB	.252	.246	.252	.000***
2.2: CB, CI	.331	.320	.079	.000***
3: CI, CB, BF	.347	.331	.016	.089*
4: CI, CB, BF, AL	.348	.326	.000	.768 (NS)
5: CI, CB, BF, AL, Iv	.384	.358	.036	.010**
6: CI, CB, BF, AL, Iv, In	.388	.356	.003	.423 (NS)
7: CI, CB, BF, AL, Iv, In, G	.392	.355	.004	.377 (NS)
8: CI, CB, BF, AL, Iv, In, G, A	.447	.408	.055	.001***

Note: * p < .1; ** p < .05; *** p < .01; NS = not significant;
WP = Willingness to Pay a Price Premium; CI = Customer Inspiration; CB = Customer Inspiration by Böttger et al. (2017); BF = Brand Familiarity; AL = Ad Liking; Iv = Involvement; In = Income; G = Gender; A = Age

Table 3.31 Results of moderation analysis with interaction terms

Moderator Variable	Independent Variable	Dependent Variable	Effect Size (f^2) of Moderator	Path Coefficient
Age	Customer Inspiration	Purchase Intention	.006	−.052 (NS)
	Customer Inspiration	Willingness to Pay	.010	.077 (NS)
Involvement	Customer Inspiration	Willingness to Pay	.027	−.123 (NS)

Note: * p < .1; ** p < .05; *** p < .01; NS = not significant

Additional Calculation

In order to understand the structure of the two predictor constructs, brand attitude and customer inspiration, we ran an exploratory factor analysis (EFA) over all items of brand attitude and customer inspiration. With this step, we wanted to analyze how the constructs correlated with each other and whether the factors of the two constructs are distinct. We used SPSS to run this calculation. The minimum sample size for an EFA was sufficient (Nunnally, 1978). The requirements for an EFA were met with a Kaiser-Meyer-Olkin index of .908 and a significant Bartlett's Test of Sphericity ($\chi^2_{91} = 1317.04$, $p < .01$). The EFA extracted two factors with an Eigenvalue above 1.000, which together explained 73.96% of the variance. The communalities (Min = .549; Max = .859) and factor loadings (Min = .691; Max = .869) were all above .500. With only one exception (CI_1), the items loaded into their corresponding factors (factor 1 = customer inspiration; factor 2 = brand attitude). We interpret these results—summarized in Table 3.32—as additional evidence that the two constructs are empirically distinct.

Table 3.32 Rotated component matrix after three iterations within EFA

Item		Factor	
		1	2
BA_1	Overall feeling of Nike ... Bad-Good	.297	**.867**
BA_2	... Pleasant-Unpleasant*	.085	**.736**
BA_3	... Dislike-Like	.323	**.869**
CI_1	I feel enthusiastic about the brand.	.494	**.691**
CI_2	I feel connected to the brand.	**.796**	.360
CI_3	I identify with the brand.	**.744**	.390
CI_4	Through the brand I experience sudden realizations.	**.812**	.279
CI_5	The brand sets me thinking.	**.745**	.064
CI_6	The brand makes me see things in a new way.	**.802**	.247
CI_7	When I think of the brand I feel full of energy.	**.836**	.327
CI_8	The brand makes me ready to take on new challenges.	**.856**	.258
CI_9	The brand makes everything feel alive.	**.868**	.285

Note: BA = Brand Attitude; CI = Customer Inspiration; * reversely coded;

Summary of Results
Overall, we replicated the outcomes from study 1 and revealed additional insights regarding the predictive relevance of customer inspiration. The assessment of the HOC of customer inspiration showed that all three components of customer inspiration contribute to the construct in absolute terms. We again found support of our hypothesis H_{1a} and H_{1b}. The results indicate that customer inspiration predicts purchase intention (PC = .595***; f^2 = .445; R^2 = .562) and willingness to pay (PC = .404***; f^2 = .162; R^2 = .447) well. We did not find any support of our hypotheses H_{2a} and H_{2b}. This could have two reasons: first, the expected higher variance among the involvement items for the different product did not occur (M_{min} = 5.24; M_{max} = 6.02; SD_{min} = 1.13; SD_{max} = 1.58) and consequently a moderating effect could not be assessed due to missing variance in the latent variable; and second, although consumer psychology studies have identified consumers' product involvement as a central factor influencing consumer behavior

(Dholakia, 2001), the level of customer inspiration might not be affected. Inspiring brands might touch, activate, and transform consumers independently from the product relevance of the individual. The brand's message as such might be the driving force for customer inspiration. Further, we found support for H_{3a} and H_{3b} as in study 1. The comparative analysis of ΔR^2 values indicated a relative higher explanatory power of customer inspiration compared with brand attitude. The same applies for the comparison of the two customer inspiration constructs. In its explanatory power, the newly-developed construct of customer inspiration exceeds the existing construct conceptualized by Böttger et al. (2017). This effect is slightly higher for the prediction of purchase intention than for the willingness to pay a price premium. Overall, H_{4a} and H_{4b} are supported.

3.5   Discussion

Market researchers are constantly exploring consumer behavior and its underlying factors. In this context, customer-brand relationships are receiving increasing attention (Fournier, 1998; Nguyen & Feng, 2020). Researchers have examined phenomena such as brand love (R. Bagozzi, Batra, & Ahuvia, 2017) and self-brand connection (Escalas & Bettman, 2003), each of which describe facets of special ways in which consumers interact with brands and integrate them in their lives. A rather new construct in this area is customer inspiration, defined as the level of identification with and activation through a brand's mindset and actions (**Study I**). In contrast to existing definitions by e.g. Böttger et al. (2017), the focal construct of this study is constituent of the three components, namely connection, transformation, and activation. Besides the conceptualization (**Study I**) and the development and validation of a measurement tool (**Study II**), the construct lacked empirical evidence that it is worth measuring. Hence, the main object of this study was to examine the question of whether the construct of customer inspiration adds value to researchers and practitioners in measuring consumer behavior compared with the well-established construct of brand attitude and compared with the existing measure of customer inspiration by Böttger et al. (2017). Beyond that, the study at hand aimed to apply the newly-developed customer inspiration scale of **Study II** as a tool to assess the level of inspiration of customers and tried to expand its nomological network. This study contributes to the stream of research exploring inspiration as a phenomenon (Hart, 1998; Thrash & Elliot, 2003) and as a valuable customer state (Böttger et al., 2017; Rudolph et al., 2012). Our study results show that 1) customer inspiration drives valuable consumer behavior intentions, 2) is distinct from the established brand attitude construct and 3) adds valuable explanatory power to purchase intention and willingness to pay a price premium compared with the brand attitude construct and the existing measure of customer inspiration. In the following, the answers to each research question are presented in detail.

RQ1:   *How does the level of customer inspiration affect willingness to pay a price premium and purchase intention?*

Previous studies have evidenced a positive effect of customer inspiration on impulse buying behavior and purchase intention (Böttger et al., 2017). As our understanding of customer inspiration differs from the authors', we wanted to reassess the effect on purchase intention and further expand the nomological network of the construct by assessing its effect on willingness to pay a price premium. The notion that customer-brand relationships can prompt a higher willingness to pay has been demonstrated within studies of emotional brand attachment (Thomson et al., 2005). Since brand relationships are understood as brand equity facets (Keller, 2001) our findings support literature evidencing willingness to pay as a summary measure of brand equity (Aaker, 1996). The results of both studies indicate that consumers who show a higher level of customer inspiration also show a higher level of purchase intention and willingness to pay a price premium. As reasons why consumers buy certain products or are willing to invest more in some brands are manifold, we controlled for the most prominent factors like brand familiarity (Monroe, 1976), ad liking (Rossiter, 2012), income, gender, and age. We interpret our results in the sense that customer inspiration is a good predictor of willingness to pay a price premium and purchase intention.

RQ2:   *How does the level of involvement with the product determine the impact of customer inspiration?*

Involvement describes how important and relevant an object is to an individual, based on his/her needs and interests (Zaichkowsky, 1985). Consumers' product involvement is a central influencing factor of consumer behavior (Dholakia, 2001) and it shapes the impact on brand evaluations (Charters & Pettigrew, 2006) and affects purchase intentions (L. Hollebeek, Jaeger, Brodie, & Balemi, 2007). In neither of our two studies could we detect an interaction effect between product involvement and customer inspiration. Hence, it seems that the level of involvement with the product does not affect the explanatory power of customer inspiration. This could have several reasons. One reason might be that the evaluated brands may have elicited relatively homogeneous levels of involvement. Since the level of involvement is always dependent on the brand or product and the audience (Rossiter & Percy, 1985), we tried to overcome the subjective involvement levels by directly asking the respondents about their level of involvement, in contrast to presenting pre-selected low- and high-involvement product-related brands. However, the chosen brands may have not covered the entire range of involvement levels, which might have detected a moderation effect. Another reason could be that the activating and transformational effect of customer inspiration unfolds independently of the product involvement levels. Since customer inspiration can also occur outside of the purchase situation, a product relevance might not be necessary to inspire consumers. It could be the case that emotional branding—characterized as a "consumer-centric, relational, and story-driven approach to forging deep and enduring affective bonds between consumers and brands" (Thompson et al., 2006, p. 50)—is independent from the product relevance. Further studies are needed to fully uncover the above-stated potential reasons. Based on our two studies, we could not find support for the notion that the level of product involvement determines the impact of customer inspiration.

RQ3:   *Which of the three predictor variables of customer inspiration, brand attitude, and customer inspiration by Böttger et al. (2017) has a higher explanatory power towards willingness to pay a price premium and purchase intention?*

The third research question aimed to investigate whether the construct of customer inspiration adds value compared with brand attitude and customer inspiration by Böttger et al. (2017) in explaining relevant outcome variables. First, we compared brand attitude and customer inspiration. Grounded on the elaboration-consistency hypothesis (R. Petty et al., 1995), we assumed a relatively higher explanatory power of customer inspiration due to its higher amount of issue-relevant thinking. The results were in line with our assumption and revealed that customer inspiration has a higher explanatory power than brand attitude for willingness to pay a price premium and purchase intention. Since previous studies emphasized that the predictive power of brand attitude is moderated by the extremity of the assessment (Park et al., 2010), we estimated the overall model with the brand attitude strength construct but did not find opposing results. Second, we compared the two existing measures of customer inspiration in terms of their explanatory power. In **Study I** and **Study II**, we argued that existing measures of customer inspiration face limitations in terms of content validity. We redefined the construct by means of the theories-in-use approach (**Study I**) and developed a new measure for customer inspiration (**Study II**). The results of this study add empirical evidence that customer inspiration has a higher explanatory power than customer inspiration by Böttger et al. (2017) towards willingness to pay a price premium and purchase intention.

Managerial Implications
With this study, we have shown that customer inspiration and brand attitude are two related but distinct constructs. As customer inspiration is a good predictor of willingness to pay a price premium and purchase intention, it is worth investing in marketing strategies that evoke customers' inspiration. Especially in a time where classic branding mechanisms are disrupted due to consumers' hyperconnectivity (Swaminathan et al., 2020), marketing managers seek for ways to win customers' attention. In order to justify a price premium in the future, it is necessary to focus on differentiating features that provide real added value for consumers. Our findings indicate that a customer's inspiration level can justify a price premium. Brands that are able to inspire consumers through emotional branding strategies (Thompson et al., 2006) can differentiate from competitors as they add value to consumers. In case companies choose to inspire customers, they should focus on three components—namely connection, transformation, and activation—and use our nine-item measure to assess the level of customer inspiration of their brands over the measure developed by Böttger et al. (2017).

Limitations and Directions for Further Research
This study also comes with some limitations. First, both studies only assess stated behavioral intentions. An assessment of actual purchasing behavior is still outstanding. Although intentions are good indicators of consumers' purchase behavior (Armstrong, Morwitz, & Kumar, 2000; Chandon, Morwitz, & Reinartz, 2005), studies also have shown that substantial differences exist between stated and actual behavior (R. P. Bagozzi & Dholakia, 1999; Jamieson & Bass, 1989). Differences can occur through either systematic biases in stated behavior (Kahneman & Snell, 1992) or through unstable correlations between intentions and behaviors (Gollwitzer, 1999). Hence, further research is needed to examine the explanatory power of customer inspiration on real actions to overcome this limitation. Other studies have shown that evaluations can be used for such a study with a mix of real market sales data and a survey that assesses brand. A potential cooperation with online retailers would be desirable and helpful at this point.

Second, with this study we have examined the explanatory power of two customer inspiration constructs and brand attitude. Conclusions about the predictive power of each variable can only partly be drawn from our analysis. The distinction between explanation and prediction seems to cause misinterpretation among scientists (Shmueli, 2011). We understand the explanatory analysis as a method to understand the data set that we conducted. Based on our theoretical model, we used this method to test our hypotheses. An analysis of the predictive power tries to extrapolate toward the unknown and offers a prediction for a future relationship. The latter is an important analysis that can be conducted through PLSpredict (Shmueli et al., 2019). Within our study, we have also reported the Q^2 value that resulted from a blindfolding procedure (Chin, 1998). Although the name itself suggests that it is an indicator of predictive power, it is not ideal as it only partly includes out-of-sample prediction (Shmueli et al., 2019). We recommend using PLSpredict in future studies to assess the predictive power of a model and overcome this limitation.

Third, as mentioned in the literature review, many drivers of purchase intention and willingness to pay a price premium exist. Although we controlled for ad- and brand-related factors such as ad liking and brand familiarity, as well as consumer-related factors like gender, income, and age, there might be confounding factors that we did not take into account and might influence our results. In addition, correlations and SEM only assess relationships but not causality. Therefore, we tried to derive our hypotheses by means of a thorough theoretical foundation as a base for our statistical analysis. Nevertheless, an experimental study design would be necessary to prove a causal relationship between customer inspiration and purchase intention, willingness to pay, or other criterion variables. Future research could think of potential experimental study designs.

Fourth, the study at hand has not uncovered the drivers of customer inspiration. For now, customer inspiration has been conceptualized (**Study I**), a measurement model has been introduced and validated (**Study II**) and the explanatory power towards future sales-oriented outcomes has been assessed and compared with the brand attitude construct and the construct conceptualized by Böttger et al. (2017) (**Study III**). The drivers of customers are still to be investigated to understand what really evokes inspiration. This shortcoming has already been addressed in other studies about the construct (Böttger et al., 2017). An early attempt to understand the drivers of customer inspiration has been made by Rudolph and Pfrang (2014), who categorize stimuli that trigger inspiration in primary and secondary sources. Whereas primary sources directly result in outcomes and additional purchases, secondary sources are suggested to only have an effect in combination with primary sources. Among the primary sources, the authors mention bundled product presentations or product-in-use visualizations. Secondary sources include music, lightening or ambient scents (Girard, Meyer, & Multani, 2013) in local stores. It is important to mention that the underlying definition of customer inspiration differs from the one used in this study. Consequently, these identified sources of inspiration might not apply in our case. Nevertheless, further research is needed to identify what really drives customer inspiration for either operationalization of the phenomenon.

Since research on customer inspiration remains in its infancy, there are several future research directions that can be taken. Besides the above-mentioned ideas, it would be interesting to uncover the role of purpose for customer inspiration. Purpose—which can also be described as a mission in life or goal orientation (Reker, 2000)—might play an important role for triggering inspiration. Research has shown that people suffer psychological difficulties if they lack a purpose in life (Frankl, 1967). Brands that can deliver their purpose towards consumers and inspire them with their goal orientation might have a competitive advantage as they are able to build a strong customer-brand relationship with their consumers. Further, it would be interesting to investigate the effect of customer inspiration on consumer well-being (Devezer, Sprott, Spangenberg, & Czellar, 2014).

Conclusion
The state of inspiration has received some attention within the psychological domain (Hart, 1998; Thrash & Elliot, 2003, 2004; Thrash, Maruskin, et al., 2010). Within the marketing literature, customer inspiration is a rather recent phenomenon, albeit which enjoys increasing attention (Böttger et al., 2017; Rauschnabel et al., 2019; Rudolph, Nagengast, & Weber, 2014; Rudolph & Pfrang, 2014). The first studies have provided evidence that customer inspiration plays a role for customer satisfaction, loyalty, and impulse buying behavior (Böttger et al., 2017). However, until recently no study has investigated how important this role is compared with the "plain vanilla" construct of brand attitude. In addition, the existing customer inspiration conceptualization faces limitations in terms of content validity. This study has sought to contribute to exploring this role by exploring the explanatory power of customer inspiration in relation to the well-established brand attitude construct. The results provide first evidence that this role is indeed an important one in explaining purchase intention and the willingness to pay a price premium for the analyzed brands of Nike and Tesla. In addition, we have provided empirical evidence that the newly-developed customer inspiration constructs are a better measure of the phenomenon of inspiration of customers than the existing measure. With this study, we wanted to show that customer inspiration is a customer-brand relationship construct that is worth investing in both marketing research and practice.

References

Aaker, D. A. (1996). Measuring Brand Equity Across Products and Markets. *California Management Review, 38*(3), 102–120.

Abdelnour, A., Babbitz, T., & Moss, S. (2020). Pricing in a Pandemic: Navigating the COVID-19 Crisis. Retrieved from https://www.mckinsey.com/business-functions/marketing-and-sales/our-insights/pricing-in-a-pandemic-navigating-the-covid-19-crisis.

Ahearne, M., Bhattacharya, C., & Gruen, T. (2005). Antecedents and Consequences of Customer—Company Identification: Expanding the Role of Relationship Marketing. *The Journal of Applied Psychology, 90*(3), 574–585.

Ailawadi, K. L., Neslin, S. A., & Lehmann, D. R. (2003). Revenue Premium as an Outcome Measure of Brand Equity. *Journal of Marketing, 67*(4), 1–17.

Ajzen, I. (1985). From Intentions to Actions: A Theory of Planned Behavior. In J. Kuhl & J. Beckmann (Eds.), *Action Control: From Cognition to Behavior* (pp. 11–39). Berlin: Springer.

Ajzen, I. (1988). *Attitudes, Personality, and Behavior*. Homewood: Dorsey Press.

Ajzen, I., & Fishbein, M. (1977). Attitude-Behavior Relations: A Theoretical Analysis and Review of Empirical Research. *Psychological Bulletin, 84*(5), 888–918.

Ajzen, I., & Gilbert Cote, N. (2008). Attitudes and the Prediction of Behavior. In W. D. Crano & R. Prislin (Eds.), *Frontiers of Social Psychology. Attitudes and Attitude Change* (pp. 289–311). New York: Psychology Press.

Aldi Sued. (2020). Inspiriert. Retrieved from https://prospekt.aldi-sued.de/as_inspiriert_0620_web/page/1.

Allen, B. P., & Potkay, C. R. (1981). On the Arbitrary Distinction between States and Traits. *Journal of Personality and Social Psychology, 41*(5), 916–928.

Allport, G. W., & Odbert, H. S. (1936). Trait-Names: A Psycho-Lexical Study. *Psychological Monographs, 47*(1), i–171.

Alperstein, N. M. (1991). Imaginary Social Relationships with Celebrities Appearing in Television Commercials. *Journal of Broadcasting & Electronic Media, 35*(1), 43–58.

Anderson, J. C., & Gerbing, D. W. (1991). Predicting the Performance of Measures in a Confirmatory Factor Analysis with a Pretest Assessment of their Substantive Validities. *76*(5), 732–740.

L. Stoll, *Providing a New Perspective on Understanding and Measuring of Customer Inspiration*, Gabler Theses, https://doi.org/10.1007/978-3-658-35894-5

Ansari, A., & Mela, C. F. (2003). E-Customization. *Journal of Marketing Research, 40*(2), 131–145.

Anselmsson, J., Bondesson, N., & Johansson, U. (2014). Brand Image and Customers' Willingness to pay a Price Premium for Food Brands. *Journal of Product and Brand Management, 23*(2), 90–102.

Arango-Muñoz, S. (2014). Metacognitive Feelings, Self-Ascriptions and Mental Actions. *Philosophical Inquieries, 2*(1), 145–162.

Arango-Muñoz, S., & Michaelian, K. (2014). Epistemic Feelings, Epistemic Emotions: Review and Introduction to the Focus Section. *Philosophical Inquiries, 2*(1), 97–122.

Armstrong, J., Morwitz, V., & Kumar, V. (2000). Sales Forecasts for Existing Consumer Products and Services: Do Purchase Intentions Contribute to Accuracy? *International Journal of Forecasting, 16*, 383–397.

Arvidsson, A., & Caliandro, A. (2016). Brand Public. *Journal of Consumer Research, 42*(5), 727–748.

Assael, H., & Keon, J. (1982). Nonsampling vs. Sampling Errors in Survey Research. *Journal of Marketing, 46*(2), 114–123.

Avolio, B. J., & Yammarino, F. J. (2013). *Transformational and Charismatic Leadership: The Road Ahead* (Vol. 10). Bingley: Emerald Group Publishing Limited.

Bagozzi, R. P., & Dholakia, U. (1999). Goal Setting and Goal Striving in Consumer Behavior. *Journal of Marketing, 63*(4), 19–32.

Bagozzi, R., Batra, R., & Ahuvia, A. (2017). Brand Love: Development and Validation of a Practical Scale. *Marketing Letters, 28*(1), 1–14.

Balabanis, G., & Chatzopoulou, E. (2019). Under the Influence of a Blogger: The Role of Information-Seeking Goals and Issue Involvement. *Psychology and Marketing, 36*(4), 342–353.

Barrett, P. (2007). Structural Equation Modelling: Adjudging Model Fit. *Personality and Individual Differences, 42*(5), 815–824.

Bass, B. M. (1985). *Leadership and Performance Beyond Expectations.* New York: Free Press.

Batra, R., & Stephens, D. (1994). Attitudinal Effects of Ad-Evoked Moods and Emotions: The Moderating Role of Motivation. *Psychology and Marketing, 11*(3), 199–215.

Batra, R., Ahuvia, A., & Bagozzi, R. P. (2012). Brand Love. *Journal of Marketing, 76*(2), 1–16.

Becker, J.-M., Klein, K., & Wetzels, M. (2012). Hierarchical Latent Variable Models in PLS-SEM: Guidelines for Using Reflective-Formative Type Models. *Long Range Planning, 45*(5–6), 359–394.

Becker, J.-M., Ringle, C., & Sarstedt, M. (2018). Estimating Moderating Effects in PLS-SEM and PLSc-SEM: Interaction Term Generation*Data Treatment. *Journal of Applied Structural Equation Modeling, 2*(2), 1–21.

Bentler, P., & Bonett, D. (1980). Significance Tests and Goodness-of-Fit in Analysis of Covariance Structures. *Psychological Bulletin, 88*(3), 588–606.

Bergkvist, L., & Rossiter, J. R. (2007). The Predictive Validity of Multiple-Item Versus Single-Item Measures of the Same Constructs. *Journal of Marketing Research, 44*(2), 175–184.

Beyoncé. (2014). 7/11. Retrieved from https://www.youtube.com/watch?v=k4YRWT_Aldo.

Bhattacharya, C. B., & Sen, S. (2003). Consumer-Company Identification: A Framework for Understanding Consumers' Relationships with Companies. *Journal of Marketing, 67*(2), 76–88.

Bianchi, F., Dupreelle, P., Krueger, F., Seara, J., Watten, D., & Willersdorf, S. (2020). Fashion's Big Reset. Retrieved from https://www.bcg.com/publications/2020/fashion-ind ustry-reset-covid.

Biehal, G., Stephens, D., & Curlo, E. (1992). Attitude Toward the Ad and Brand Choice. *Journal of Advertising, 21*(3), 19–36.

Bollen, K. A., & Lennox, R. (1991). Conventional Wisdom on Measurement: A Structural Equation Perspective. *Psychological Bulletin, 110*(2), 305–314.

Bolton, R. N. (1993). Pretesting Questionnaires: Content Analyses of Respondents' Concurrent Verbal Protocols. *Marketing Science, 12*(3), 280.

Bolton, R., & Saxena-Iyer, S. (2009). Interactive Services: A Framework, Synthesis and Research Directions. *Journal of Interactive Marketing, 23*(1), 91–104.

Bosch. (2020). Kundeninspiration. Retrieved from https://kitchen.bosch-home.com/de/inspir ator/.

Böttger, T. (2015). *Inspiration in Marketing: Foundations, Process, and Application.* (Doctoral dissertation), University of St. Gallen, Difo Druck GmbH.

Böttger, T. (2019). What Drives Customer Inspiration? A Goal-Systemic Perspective. *Behavioral Marketing eJournal.* Retrieved from https://ssrn.com/abstract=3422192.

Böttger, T., Rudolph, T., Evanschitzky, H., & Pfrang, T. (2017). Customer Inspiration: Conceptualization, Scale Development, and Validation. *Journal of Marketing, 81*(6), 116–131.

Bowden, E., Beeman, M., Fleck, J., & Kounios, J. (2005). New Approaches to Demystifying Insight. *Trends in cognitive sciences, 9*(7), 322–328.

Bowlby, J. (1977). The Making and Breaking of Affectional Bonds: I. Aetiology and Psychopathology in the Light of Attachment Theory. *British Journal of Psychiatry, 130*(3), 201–210.

Bowra, C. M. (1955). *Inspiration & Poetry.* New York: Macmillan.

Bradley, H. D. (1929). *The Wisdom Of The Gods.* London: T.Werner Laurie.

Brady, M. K., Voorhees, C. M., & Brusco, M. J. (2012). Service Sweethearting: Its Antecedents and Customer Consequences. *76*(2), 81–98.

Breugelmans, E., & Campo, K. (2011). Effectiveness of In-Store Displays in a Virtual Store Environment. *Journal of Retailing, 87*(1), 75–89.

Brodie, R. J., Hollebeek, L. D., Jurić, B., & Ilić, A. (2011). Customer Engagement: Conceptual Domain, Fundamental Propositions, and Implications for Research. *Journal of Service Research, 14*(3), 252–271.

Brodie, R. J., Ilic, A., Juric, B., & Hollebeek, L. (2013). Consumer Engagement in a Virtual Brand Community: An Exploratory Analysis. *Journal of Business Research, 66*(1), 105–114.

Brooks, C. (2016). How the Global Fortune 500 Develop Marketing Strategy in a 'VUCA' World. Retrieved from https://www.the-gma.com/marketing-strategy.

Bruce, N. I., Becker, M., & Reinartz, W. (2020). Communicating Brands in Television Advertising. *Journal of Marketing Research, 57*(2), 236–256.

Bruhn, M., & Meffert, H. (2002). *Exzellenz im Dienstleistungsmarketing: Fallstudien zur Kundenorientierung.* Wiesbaden: Gabler Verlag.

Bruhn, M., Schoenmüller, V., Schäfer, D., & Heinrich, D. (2012). Brand Authenticity: Towards a Deeper Understanding of Its Conceptualization and Measurement. *Advances in consumer research., 40*, 567–576.

Bycio, P., Hackett, R. D., & Allen, J. S. (1995). Further Assessments of Bass's (1985) Conceptualization of Transactional and Transformational Leadership. *Journal of Applied Psychology, 80*(4), 468–478.

Calder, B. J., & Malthouse, E. C. (2010). Media Engagement and Advertising Effectiveness. In B. J. Calder (Ed.), *Kellogg on Advertising & Media* (pp. 1–36). Hoboken: Wiley.

Calder, B., Isaac, M., & Malthouse, E. (2015). How to Capture Consumer Experiences: A Context-Specific Approach To Measuring Engagement: Predicting Consumer Behavior Across Qualitatively Different Experiences. *Journal of Advertising Research, 56*(1), 39–52.

Campbell, M. C., Inman, J. J., Kirmani, A., & Price, L. L. (2020). In Times of Trouble: A Framework for Understanding Consumers' Responses to Threats. *Journal of Consumer Research, 47*(3), 311–326.

Campbell, M. C., Keller, K. L., Mick, D. G., & Hoyer, W. D. (2003). Brand Familiarity and Advertising Repetition Effects. *Journal of Consumer Research, 30*(2), 292–304.

Campillo-Lundbeck, S. (2020). Edeka Rührt mit Corona-Weihnachtsgeschichte um einen Alten Mann zu Tränen. Retrieved from https://www.horizont.net/marketing/nachrichten/jung-von-matt-edeka-ruehrt-mit-corona-weihnachtsgeschichte-um-einen-alten-mann-zu-traenen-187994.

Carmines, E., & Mciver, C. (1981). Analyzing Models with Unobserved Variables: Analysis of Covariance Structures. In G. W. Bohrnstedt & E. F. Borgatta (Eds.), *Social Measurement: Current Issues* (pp. 65–115). Beverly Hills: Sage Publications.

Carroll, B., & Ahuvia, A. (2006). Some Antecedents and Outcomes of Brand Love. *Marketing Letters, 17*(2), 79–89.

Celsi, R. L., & Olson, J. C. (1988). The Role of Involvement in Attention and Comprehension Processes. *Journal of Consumer Research, 15*(2), 210–224.

Cenfetelli, R., & Bassellier, G. (2009). Interpretation of Formative Measurement in Information Systems Research. *MIS Quarterly, 33*(4), 689–708.

Chakravarty, A., Kumar, A., & Grewal, R. (2014). Customer Orientation Structure for Internet-Based Business-to-Business Platform Firms. *Journal of Marketing, 78*(5), 1–23.

Chandon, P., Morwitz, V., & Reinartz, W. (2005). Do Intentions Really Predict Behavior? Self-Generated Validity Effects in Survey Research. *Journal of Marketing, 69*(2), 1–14.

Chaplin, L., & John, D. (2005). The Development of Self-Brand Connections in Children and Adolescents. *Journal of Consumer Research, 32*(1), 119–129.

Charters, S., & Pettigrew, S. (2006). Product involvement and the evaluation of wine quality. *Qualitative Market Research: An International Journal, 9*(2), 181–193.

Chaudhuri, A., & Holbrook, M. B. (2001). The Chain of Effects from Brand Trust and Brand Affect to Brand Performance: The Role of Brand Loyalty. *65*(2), 81–93.

Cheung, J., Burns, D., Sinclair, R., & Sliter, M. (2017). Amazon Mechanical Turk in Organizational Psychology: An Evaluation and Practical Recommendations. *Journal of Business & Psychology, 32*(4), 347–361.

Chin, W. W. (1998). The Partial Least Squares Approach to Structural Equation Modeling. In G. A. Marcoulides (Ed.), Methodology for Business and Management. Modern Methods for Business Research (pp. 295–336). New Jersey: Lawrence Erlbaum Associates Publishers.

Clark, T. (1997). *The Theory of Inspiration Composition as a Crisis of Subjectivity in Romantic and Post-Romantic Writing.* Manchester: University Press.

Clarke, P. (2020). Eminem Responds to Barack Obama's Dramatic Reading of 'Lose Yourself'. Retrieved from https://www.nme.com/en_asia/news/music/eminem-responds-to-barack-obamas-dramatic-reading-of-lose-yourself-2838769.

Cobb-Walgren, C., Ruble, C., & Donthu, N. (2013). Brand Equity, Brand Preference, and Purchase Intent. *Journal of Advertising, 24*(3), 25–40.

Cohen, J. (1988). *Statistical Power Analysis for the Behavioral Sciences.* Hillsdale: Elsevier Science.

Cohen, J., & Areni, C. (1991). Affect and Consumer Behavior. In T. S. Robertson & H. H. Kassarjian (Eds.), *Handbook of Consumer Behavior* (pp. 188–240). Englewood Cliffs: Prentice-Hall.

Conger, J. A., & Kanungo, R. N. (1987). Toward a Behavioral Theory of Charismatic Leadership in Organizational Settings. *Academy of Management Review, 12*(4), 637–647.

Conger, J. A., & Kanungo, R. N. (1992). Perceived Behavioural Attributes of Charismatic Leadership. *Canadian Journal of Behavioural Science, 24*(1), 86–102.

Cortina, J. (1993). What Is Coefficient Alpha? An Examination of Theory and Applications. *Journal of Applied Psychology, 78*(1), 98–104.

Cronbach, L. J., & Meehl, P. E. (1955). Construct Validity in Psychological Tests. *Psychological Bulletin, 52*(4), 281–302.

Davitz, J. R. (1969). *The Language of Emotion.* London: Elsevier Science.

Devezer, B., Sprott, D. E., Spangenberg, E. R., & Czellar, S. (2014). Consumer Well-Being: Effects of Subgoal Failures and Goal Importance. *Journal of Marketing, 78*(2), 118–134.

Dhar, R., & Wertenbroch, K. (2000). Consumer Choice Between Hedonic and Utilitarian Goods. *Journal of Marketing Research, 37*(1), 60–71.

Dholakia, U. (2001). A Motivational Process Model of Product Involvement and Consumer Risk Perception. *European Journal of Marketing, 35*(11–12), 1340–1362.

Diamantopoulos, A. (2005). The C-OAR-SE Procedure for Scale Development in Marketing: a Comment. *International Journal of Research in Marketing, 22*(1), 1–9.

Diamantopoulos, A., & Winklhofer, H. M. (2001). Index Construction with Formative Indicators: An Alternative to Scale Development. *Journal of Marketing Research (JMR), 38*(2), 269–277.

Diener, E., Heintzelman, S., Kushlev, K., Tay, L., Wirtz, D., Lutes, L., & Oishi, S. (2016). Findings All Psychologists Should Know From the New Science on Subjective Well-Being. *Canadian Psychology, 58*(2), 87–104.

Dion, D., & Borraz, S. (2017). Managing Status: How Luxury Brands Shape Class Subjectivities in the Service Encounter. *Journal of Marketing, 81*(5), 67–85.

Douglas, S. P., & Craig, C. S. (2007). Collaborative and Iterative Translation: An Alternative Approach to Back Translation. *Journal of International Marketing, 15*(1), 30–43.

Dumouchel, L., & Kahn, Z. (2020). Brand Growth in Times of Crises. Retrieved from https://www.ipsos.com/en/brand-growth-times-crisis.

Dwivedi, A., Nayeem, T., & Murshed, F. (2018). Brand Experience and Consumers' Willingness-To-Pay (WTP) a Price Premium: Mediating Role of Brand Credibility and Perceived Uniqueness. *Journal of Retailing and Consumer Services, 44*(1), 100–107.

Efklides, A. (2006). Metacognition and Affect: What can Metacognitive Experiences tell us About the Learning Process? *Educational Research Review, 1*(1), 3–14.

Eggert, A., Steinhoff, L., & Witte, C. (2019). Gift Purchases as Catalysts for Strengthening Customer–Brand Relationships. *Journal of Marketing, 83*(5), 115–132.

Eliade, M., & Adams, C. J. (1987). *The Encyclopedia of Religion*. London: MacMillan.

Engelmann, B. (2006). Measures of a Rating's Discriminative Power—Applications and Limitations. In B. Engelmann & R. Rauhmeier (Eds.), *The Basel II Risk Parameters: Estimation, Validation, and Stress Testing* (pp. 263–287). Berlin: Springer.

Erdem, T., & Swait, J. (1998). Brand Equity as a Signaling Phenomenon. *Journal of Consumer Psychology, 7*(2), 131–157.

Escalas, J. E. (2004). Narrative Processing: Building Consumer Connections to Brands. *Journal of Consumer Psychology, 14*(1/2), 168–180.

Escalas, J. E., & Bettman, J. R. (2003). You Are What They Eat: The Influence of Reference Groups on Consumers' Connections to Brands. *Journal of Consumer Psychology, 13*(3), 339.

Fazio, R. H. (1990). Multiple Processes by which Attitudes Guide Behavior: The Mode Model as an Integrative Framework. In M. P. Zanna (Ed.), *Advances in Experimental Social Psychology* (Vol. 23, pp. 75–109). New York: Academic Press.

Fazio, R. H. (1995). Attitudes as Object-Evaluation Associations: Determinants, Consequences, and Correlates of Attitude Accessibility. In R. E. Petty & J. A. Krosnick (Eds.), *Attitude Strength: Antecedents and Consequences.* (pp. 247–282). Hillsdale: Lawrence Erlbaum Associates.

Fernandes, T., & Remelhe, P. (2016). How to Engage Customers in Co-Creation: Customers' Motivations for Collaborative Innovation. *Journal of Strategic Marketing, 24*(3/4), 311–326.

Festge, F., & Schwaiger, M. (2007). The Drivers of Customer Satisfaction with Industrial Goods: An International Study. *Advances in International Marketing, 18*, 179–207.

Fetscherin, M., & Heinrich, D. (2015). Consumer Brand Relationships Research: A Bibliometric Citation Meta-Analysis. *Journal of Business Research, 68*(2), 380–390.

Fischer, M., Völckner, F., & Sattler, H. (2010). How Important Are Brands? A Cross-Category, Cross-Country Study. *Journal of Marketing Research, 47*(5), 823–839.

Fishbein, M., & Ajzen, I. (1975). *Belief, Attitude, Intention and Behaviour: An Introduction to Theory and Research*. Reading: Addison-Wesley.

Flick, U. (2007). *Qualitative Sozialforschung: Eine Einführung*. Berlin: Rowohlt-Taschenbuch-Verlag.

Fornell, C., & Cha, J. (1994). Partial Least Squares. *Advanced Methods of Marketing Research, 407*, 52–78.

Fornell, C., & Larcker, D. F. (1981). Evaluating Structural Equation Models with Unobservable Variables and Measurement Error. *Journal of Marketing Research, 18*(1), 39–50.

Fournier, S. (1998). Consumers and Their Brands: Developing Relationship Theory in Consumer Research. *Journal of Consumer Research, 24*(4), 343–373.

Frankl, V. E. (1967). Logotherapy and Existentialism. *Psychotherapy: Theory, Research & Practice, 4*(3), 138–142.

Galoni, C., Carpenter, G. S., & Rao, H. (2020). Disgusted and Afraid: Consumer Choices under the Threat of Contagious Disease. *Journal of Consumer Research, 47*(3), 373–392.

Gambetti, R., & Graffigna, G. (2010). The Concept of Engagement: A Systematic Analysis of the Ongoing Marketing Debate. *International Journal of Market Research, 52*(6), 801–826.

Gardner, M. P. (1985). Does Attitude toward the Ad Affect Brand Attitude under a Brand Evaluation Set? *Journal of Marketing Research, 22*(2), 192–198.

Gavilanes, J. M., Flatten, T. C., & Brettel, M. (2018). Content Strategies for Digital Consumer Engagement in Social Networks: Why Advertising Is an Antecedent of Engagement. *Journal of Advertising, 47*(1), 4–23.

Giner-Sorolla, R. (1999). Affect in Attitude: Immediate and Deliberative Perspectives. In *Dual-Process Theories in Social Psychology* (pp. 441–461). New York: Guilford Press.

Girard, M., Meyer, A., & Multani, A. (2013). *The Long-Term Impact of Ambient Scents in the Service Environment on Customers.* Paper presented at the 22th Annual Frontiers in Service Conference, Taipei, Taiwan.

Glaser, B. G., & Strauss, A. L. (1967). *The Discovery of Grounded Theory: Strategies for Qualitative Research.* London: Aldine.

Goldsmith, R. E., & Emmert, J. (1991). Measuring Product Category Involvement: A Multitrait-Multimethod study. *Journal of Business Research, 23*(4), 363–371.

Gollwitzer, P. M. (1999). Implementation Intentions: Strong Effects of Simple Plans. *American Psychologist, 54*(7), 493–503.

Goodman, J. K., Cryder, C. E., & Cheema, A. (2013). Data Collection in a Flat World: The Strengths and Weaknesses of Mechanical Turk Samples. *Journal of Behavioral Decision Making, 26*(3), 213–224.

GoPro. (2019). Ignite Your Creativity. Retrieved from https://www.youtube.com/watch?v=jMUEWM45i-0.

GoPro. (2020). About us. Retrieved from https://gopro.com/en/us/about-us.

Greenwald, A. G., Banaji, M. R., Rudman, L. A., Farnham, S. D., Nosek, B. A., & Mellott, D. S. (2002). A Unified Theory of Implicit Attitudes, Stereotypes, Self-Esteem, and Self-Concept. *Psychological Review, 109*(1), 3–25.

Groth, M. (2005). Customers as Good Soldiers: Examining Citizenship Behaviors in Internet Service Deliveries. *Journal of Management, 31*(1), 7–27.

Groves, A. M. (2001). Authentic British Food Products: A Review of Consumer Perceptions. *International Journal of Consumer Studies, 25*(3), 246–254.

Hair, J. F., Black, W. C., Babin, B. J., & Anderson, R. E. (2010). *Multivariate Data Analysis.* Upper Saddle River: Pearson Education.

Hair, J. F., Hult, T., Ringle, C., & Sarstedt, M. (2014). *A Primer on Partial Least Squares Structural Equation Modeling.* Thousand Oaks: Sage Publications.

Handelsblatt. (2019). Weihnachtsgeschäft Bringt GoPro in Schwarze Zahlen Zurück. *Handelsblatt.* Retrieved from https://www.handelsblatt.com/unternehmen/handel-konsumgueter/actionkamera-hersteller-weihnachtsgeschaeft-bringt-gopro-in-schwarze-zahlen-zurueck/23958936.html?ticket=ST-8504884-w2PSy0pcKja6tYlwVgbJ-ap5.

Hart, T. (1998). Inspiration: Exploring the Experience and its Meaning. *Journal of Humanistic Psychology, 38*(3), 7–35.

Haynes, S., Richard, D., & Kubany, E. (1995). Content Validity in Psychological Assessment: A Functional Approach to Concepts and Methods. *Psychological Assessment, 7*(3), 238–247.

He, Y., Chen, Q., & Alden, D. (2016). Time Will Tell: Managing Post-Purchase Changes in Brand Attitude. *Journal of the Academy of Marketing Science, 44*(6), 791–805.

Henseler, J. (2017). Bridging Design and Behavioral Research With Variance-Based Structural Equation Modeling. *Journal of Advertising, 46*(1), 178–192.

Henseler, J., Ringle, C., & Sarstedt, M. (2015). A New Criterion for Assessing Discriminant Validity in Variance-based Structural Equation Modeling. *Journal of the Academy of Marketing Science, 43*(1), 115–135.

Higgins, E. T. (2006). Value From Hedonic Experience and Engagement. *Psychological Review, 113*(3), 439–460.

Hinkin, T. R. (1995). A Review of Scale Development Practices in the Study of Organizations. *Journal of Management, 21*(5), 967–988.

Hirschman, E. C. (1994). Consumers and Their Animal Companions. *Journal of Consumer Research, 20*(4), 616–632.

Hoch, S. J. (2002). Product Experience Is Seductive. *Journal of Consumer Research, 29*(3), 448–454.

Hollebeek, L. (2011). Exploring Customer Brand Engagement: Definition and Themes. *Journal of Strategic Marketing, 19*(7), 555–573.

Hollebeek, L. (2011a). Demystifying Customer Brand Engagement: Exploring the Loyalty Nexus. *Journal of Marketing Management, 27*(7–8), 785–807.

Hollebeek, L. (2011b). Exploring Customer Brand Engagement: Definition and Themes. *Journal of Strategic Marketing, 19*(7), 555–573.

Hollebeek, L., Glynn, M., & Brodie, R. (2014). Consumer Brand Engagement in Social Media: Conceptualization, Scale Development and Validation. *Journal of Interactive Marketing, 28*(2), 149–165.

Hollebeek, L., Jaeger, S., Brodie, R., & Balemi, A. (2007). The Influence of Involvement on Purchase Intention for New World Wine. *Food Quality and Preference, 18*(8), 1033–1049.

Homburg, C., Wieseke, J., & Hoyer, W. (2009). Social Identity and the Service-Profit Chain. *Journal of Marketing, 73*(2), 38–54.

Howell, J. M., & Shamir, B. (2005). The Role of Followers in the Charismatic Leadership Process: Relationships and their Consequences. *Academy of Management Review, 30*(1), 96–112.

Hung, I. W., & Wyer, R. S. (2011). Shaping Consumer Imaginations: The Role of Self-Focused Attention in Product Evaluations. *Journal of Marketing Research, 48*(2), 381–392.

Hunt, N. C., & Scheetz, A. M. (2019). Using MTurk to Distribute a Survey or Experiment: Methodological Considerations. *Journal of Information Systems, 33*(1), 43–65.

Hymer, S. (1990). On Inspiration. *The Psychotherapy Patient, 6*(3–4), 17–38.

Ikea. (2020). Rooms Inspiration. Retrieved from https://www.ikea.com/de/de/rooms-inspiration/.

Izogo, E., Mpinganjira, M., & Ogba, F. (2020). Does the Collectivism/Individualism Cultural Orientation determine the effect of Customer Inspiration on Customer Citizenship Behaviors? *Journal of Hospitality and Tourism Management, 43*, 190–198.

Jamieson, L. F., & Bass, F. M. (1989). Adjusting Stated Intention Measures to Predict Trial Purchase of New Products: A Comparison of Models and Methods. *Journal of Marketing Research, 26*(3), 336–345.

Jarvis, C. B., Mackenzie, S. B., Podsakoff, P. M., Mick, D. G., & Bearden, W. O. (2003). A Critical Review of Construct Indicators and Measurement Model Misspecification in Marketing and Consumer Research. *Journal of Consumer Research, 30*(2), 199–218.

Johnson, J., & Sohi, R. (2016). Understanding and resolving major contractual breaches in buyer-seller relationships: a grounded theory approach. *Journal of the Academy of Marketing Science, 44*(2), 185–205.

Jöreskog, K., & Goldberger, A. (1975). Estimation of a Model with Multiple Indicators and Multiple Causes of a Single Latent Variable. *Journal of the American Statistical Association, 70*(315), 631–639.

Kahneman, D., & Snell, J. (1992). Predicting a Changing taste: Do People Know What They Will Like? *Journal of Behavioral Decision Making, 5*(3), 187–200.

Kantar. (2019). Best of BrandZ 2019. Retrieved from https://www.kantar.com/campaigns/bra ndz/global/.

Kantar. (2020). Brand Equity. Retrieved from https://www.kantar.com/expertise/brand-gro wth/brand-performance-tracking-and-equity/brand-equity/.

Kapferer, J. N. (2008). *The New Strategic Brand Management: Creating and Sustaining Brand Equity Long Term*. London: Kogan Page.

Kees, J., Berry, C., Burton, S., & Sheehan, K. (2017). An Analysis of Data Quality: Professional Panels, Student Subject Pools, and Amazon's Mechanical Turk. *Journal of Advertising, 46*(1), 141–155.

Keller, K. L. (1993). Conceptualizing, Measuring, Managing Customer-Based Brand Equity. *Journal of Marketing, 57*(1), 1–22.

Keller, K. L. (2001). Building Customer-Based Brand Equity. *Marketing Management, 10*(2), 14–19.

Keller, K. L. (2020). Consumer Research Insights on Brands and Branding: A JCR Curation. *Journal of Consumer Research, 46*(5), 995–1001.

Keller, K. L., & Lehmann, D. (2006). Brands and Branding: Research Findings and Future Priorities. *Marketing Science, 25*, 740–759.

Kennick, W. E. (1985). Art and Inauthenticity. *The Journal of Aesthetics and Art Criticism, 44*(1), 3–12.

Khamitov, M., Wang, X., & Thomson, M. (2019). How Well Do Consumer-Brand Relationships Drive Customer Brand Loyalty? Generalizations from a Meta-Analysis of Brand Relationship Elasticities. *Journal of Consumer Research, 46*(3), 435–459.

Khan, B. (2009). Operationalising Young and Rubicam's BAV as a consumer-based brand equity measure. *International Business Entrepreneurship Development, 4*, 314–333.

Kim, J., Baek, Y., & Choi, Y. H. (2012). The Structural Effects of Metaphor-Elicited Cognitive and Affective Elaboration Levels on Attitude Toward the Ad. *Journal of Advertising, 41*(2), 77–96.

Kim, J., Morris, J. D., & Swait, J. (2008). Antecedents of True Brand Loyalty. *Journal of Advertising, 37*(2), 99–117.

Koschate-Fischer, N., Stefan, I. V., & Hoyer, W. D. (2012). Willingness to Pay for Cause-Related Marketing: The Impact of Donation Amount and Moderating Effects. *Journal of Marketing Research, 49*(6), 910–927.

Kotler, P., Kartajaya, H., Setiawan, I., & Pyka, P. (2017). *Marketing 4.0: Der Leitfaden für das Marketing der Zukunft*. Frankfurt am Main: Campus Verlag.

Kroeber-Riel, W. (1979). Activation Research: Psychobiological Approaches in Consumer Research. *Journal of Consumer Research, 5*(4), 240–250.

Krosnick, J., Boninger, D., Chuang, Y. C., Berent, M., & Carnot, C. (1993). Attitude Strength: One Construct or Many Related Constructs? *Journal of Personality and Social Psychology, 65*(6), 1132–1151.

Krupić, D., Banai, B., & Corr, P. J. (2018). Relations Between the Behavioral Approach System (BAS) and Self-Reported Life History Traits. *Journal of Individual Differences, 39*(2), 115–122.

Kumar, V., & Pansari, A. (2016). Competitive Advantage Through Engagement. *Journal of Marketing Research, 53*(4), 497–514.

Kumar, V., & Reinartz, W. (2016). Creating Enduring Customer Value. *Journal of Marketing, 80*(6), 36–68.

Kwon, J., & Boger, C. A. (2020). Influence of Brand Experience on Customer Inspiration and Pro-Environmental Intention. *Current Issues in Tourism*, 1–15.

Landfester, M., Cancik, H., & Schneider, H. (2006). *Brill's New Pauly: Encyclopaedia of the Ancient World*. Leiden: Brill.

Lego. (2019). The LEGO Group Annual Report 2019. Retrieved from https://www.lego.com/cdn/cs/aboutus/assets/blt55a9aaa4253b2fa5/Annual_Report_2019_ENG.pdf.pdf.

Lego. (2020). Retrieved from https://www.lego.com/de-de/aboutus.

Leippe, M. R., & Elkin, R. A. (1987). When Motives Clash: Issue Involvement and Response Involvement as Determinants of Persuasion. *Journal of Personality and Social Psychology, 52*(2), 269–278.

Levine, B. (2019). Budweiser's 'Serve Our Heroes' Tops Ranking of Purpose-Driven Ads. *MarketingDive*. Retrieved from https://www.marketingdive.com/news/budweisers-serve-our-heroes-tops-ranking-of-purpose-driven-ads/562864/

Levy, S. J. (1959). The Status Seekers by Vance Packard. *Journal of Marketing, 24*(2), 121–122.

Lockwood, P., & Kunda, Z. (1997). Superstars and Me: Predicting the Impact of Role Models on the Self. *Journal of Personality and Social Psychology, 73*(1), 91–103.

Lockwood, P., Jordan, C., & Kunda, Z. (2002). Motivation by Positive or Negative Role Models: Regulatory Focus Determines Who Will Best Inspire Us. *Journal of Personality and Social Psychology, 83*(4), 854–864.

Luckwaldt, S. (2020). Wie Mark Bezner die Modefirma Olymp durch die Krise Steuert. Retrieved from https://www.capital.de/leben/um-schaden-von-olymp-abzuwenden-gaebe-ich-mein-letztes-hemd.

Lutz, R. J. (1975). Changing Brand Attitudes Through Modification of Cognitive Structure. *Journal of Consumer Research, 1*(4), 49–59.

Lutz, R. J., McKenzie, S. B., & Belch, G. E. (1983). Attitude Toward the Ad as a Mediator of Advertising Effectiveness: Determinants and Consequences. *Advances in Consumer Research, 10*(1), 532–539.

MacKenzie, S. B., Lutz, R. J., & Belch, G. E. (1986). The Role of Attitude Toward the Ad as a Mediator of Advertising Effectiveness: A Test of Competing Explanations. *Journal of Marketing Research, 23*(2), 130–143.

Malär, L., Krohmer, H., Hoyer, W. D., & Nyffenegger, B. (2011). Emotional Brand Attachment and Brand Personality: The Relative Importance of the Actual and the Ideal Self. *Journal of Marketing, 75*(4), 35–52.

Marketing Science Institute. (2010). *Marketing Science Institute 2010–2012 Research Priorities.* Cambridg: Marketing Science Institute.

Maybelline. (2020). Nude Makeup Inspiration. Retrieved from https://www.maybelline.com/makeup-trends/nudes-makeup.

Mayring, P., & Fenzl, T. (2014). Qualitative Inhaltsanalyse. In N. Baur & J. Blasius (Eds.), *Handbuch Methoden der empirischen Sozialforschung* (pp. 543–556). Wiesbaden: Springer Fachmedien.

Meffert, H., Bruhn, M., & Hadwich, K. (2018). *Dienstleistungsmarketing: Grundlagen—Konzepte—Methoden.* Wiesbaden: Springer Fachmedien.

Mende, M., Bolton, R. N., & Bitner, M. J. (2013). Decoding Customer-Firm Relationships: How Attachment Styles Help Explain Customers' Preferences for Closeness, Repurchase Intentions, and Changes in Relationship Breadth. *Journal of Marketing Research, 50*(1), 125–142.

Merriam-Webster. (2018). 'Inspire'. Retrieved from https://www.merriam-webster.com/words-at-play/the-origins-of-inspire.

Mitchell, A. A., & Olson, J. C. (1981). Are Product Attribute Beliefs the only Mediator of Advertising Effects on Brand Attitude? *Journal of Marketing Research, 18*(3), 318–332.

Mittal, B. (2006). I, Me, and Mine—How Products Become Consumers' Extended Selves. *5*(6), 550–562.

Mittal, B. (2006). I, Me, and Mine—How Products Become Consumers' Extended Selves. *Journal of Consumer Behaviour, 5*(6), 550–562.

Monroe, K. B. (1976). The Influence of Price Differences and Brand Familiarity on Brand Preferences. *Journal of Consumer Research, 3*(1), 42–49.

Morgan, N. A., & Rego, L. L. (2006). The Value of Different Customer Satisfaction and Loyalty Metrics in Predicting Business Performance. *Marketing Science, 25*(5), 426–439.

Morgan, R., & Hunt, S. (1994). The Commitment-Trust Theory of Relationship Marketing. *Journal of Marketing, 58*(3), 20–38.

Murray, P. (1981). Poetic Inspiration in Early Greece. *The Journal of Hellenic Studies, 101*, 87–100.

Needham, P. (2020). Tourism Industry Hopes for Comeback After 2020 Crash. Retrieved from https://www.fvw.de/international/travel-news/corona-impact-german-tourism-industry-hopes-for-comeback-after-2020-crash-213922?crefresh=1.

Nelson, P. (1970). Information and Consumer Behavior. *Journal of Political Economy, 78*(2), 311–329.

Neosperience. (2018). How Customers Find Ideas and Inspiration. Retrieved from https://www.neosperience.com/blog/how-customers-find-ideas-and-inspiration-infographic/

Netemeyer, R., Krishnan, B., Pullig, C., Wang, G., Yagci, M., Dean, D., . . . Wirth, F. (2004). Developing and Validating Measures of Facets of Customer-Based Brand Equity. *Journal of Business Research, 57*(2), 209–224.

Neuberger, O. (1974). *Messung der Arbeitszufriedenheit: Verfahren und Ergebnisse.* Stuttgart: Kohlhammer.

Nguyen, H. T., & Feng, H. (2020). Antecedents and Financial Impacts of Building Brand Love. *International Journal of Research in Marketing, forthcoming.*

Nicholson, R. (2014). Beyoncé's 7/11 Video: Carefully Cultivated Candour. Retrieved from https://www.theguardian.com/music/musicblog/2014/nov/24/beyonces-711-video-carefully-cultivated-candour.

Nike. (2018). Dream Crazy. Retrieved from https://www.youtube.com/watch?v=gtPdPy pgjmY.

Nunnally, J. C. (1978). *Psychometric theory*. New York: McGraw-Hill.

Obama, B. (2020). *A Promised Land*. New York: Crown Publishing Group.

O'Donnell, M., & Evers, E. R. K. (2019). Preference Reversals in Willingness to Pay and Choice. *Journal of Consumer Research, 45*(6), 1315–1330.

Oleynick, V., Thrash, T., Lefew, M., Moldovan, E., & Kieffaber, P. (2014). The Scientific Study of Inspiration in the Creative Process: Challenges and Opportunities. *Frontiers in Human Neuroscience, 8*, 1–8.

Oliver, R. L. (1999). Whence Consumer Loyalty? *Journal of Marketing, 63*, 33–44.

Oliver, R. L., & Rust, R. T. (1997). Customer Delight: Foundations, Findings, and Managerial Insight. *Journal of Retailing, 73*(3), 311–336.

Oxford English Dictionary. (Ed.) (1989). New York: Oxford University Press.

Oxford English Dictionary. (Ed.) (2019). Oxford: Oxford University Press.

Ozer, S., Oyman, M., & Ugurhan, Y. Z. C. (2020). The Surprise Effect of Ambient Ad on the Path Leading to Purchase: Testing the Role of Attitude Toward the Brand. *Journal of Marketing Communications, 26*(6), 615–635.

Palmatier, R. W., Dant, R. P., Grewal, D., & Evans, K. R. (2006). Factors Influencing the Effectiveness of Relationship Marketing: A Meta-Analysis. *Journal of Marketing, 70*(4), 136–153.

Pansari, A., & Kumar, V. (2017). Customer Engagement: The Construct, Antecedents, and Consequences. *Journal of the Academy of Marketing Science, 45*(3), 294–311.

Park, C. W., & Macinnis, D. J. (2006). What's In and What's Out: Questions on the Boundaries of the Attitude Construct. *Journal of Consumer Research, 33*(1), 16–18.

Park, C. W., Eisingerich, A. B., & Park, J. W. (2013). Attachment–Aversion (AA) Model of Customer–Brand Relationships. *Journal of Consumer Psychology, 23*(2), 229–248.

Park, C. W., MacInnis, D. J., Priester, J. R., Eisingerich, A. B., & Iacobucci, D. (2010). Brand Attachment and Brand Attitude Strength: Conceptual and Empirical Differentiation of Two Critical Brand Equity Drivers. *Journal of Marketing, 74*(6), 1–17.

Patterson, P., & Yu, T. (2006, 01/01). *Understanding Customer Engagement in Services*. Paper presented at the ANZMAC 2006 Conference, Brisbane, Australia.

Pee, L. (2016). Customer Co-Creation in B2C E-Commerce: Does it Lead to Better New Products? *Electronic Commerce Research, 16*(2), 217–243.

Petty, R. E., Cacioppo, J. T., & Schumann, D. (1983). Central and Peripheral Routes to Advertising Effectiveness: The Moderating Role of Involvement. *Journal of Consumer Research, 10*(2), 135–146.

Petty, R., Briñol, P., & Demarree, K. (2007). The Meta–Cognitive Model (MCM) of Attitudes: Implications for Attitude Measurement, Change, and Strength. *Social Cognition, 25*, 657–686.

Petty, R., Haugtvedt, C., & Smith, S. (1995). Elaboration as a Determinant of Attitude Strength: Creating Attitudes that are Persistent, Resistant, and Predictive of Behavior. In R. E. Petty & J. A. Krosnick (Eds.), *Attitude Strength: Antecedents and Consequences* (pp. 93–130). New Jersey: Lawrence Erlbaum Associates.

Phillips, B. J., & McQuarrie, E. F. (2010). Narrative and Persuasion in Fashion Advertising. *Journal of Consumer Research, 37*(3), 368–392.

Pinterest. (2020). Your Inspiring Ideas Belong Here. Retrieved from https://business.pinterest.com/en/.

Prahalad, C. K., & Ramaswamy, V. (2004). Co-Creating Unique Value With Customers. *Strategy & Leadership, 32*(3), 4–9.

Prentice, C., Han, X., Hua, L.-L., & Hu, L. (2019). The Influence of Identity-Driven Customer Engagement on Purchase Intention. *Journal of Retailing and Consumer Services, 47*, 339–347.

Priester, J. R., Nayakankuppam, D., Fleming, M. A., & Godek, J. (2004). The A2SC2 Model: The Influence of Attitudes and Attitude Strength on Consideration and Choice. *Journal of Consumer Research, 30*(4), 574–587.

Privette, G. (1983). Peak Experience, Peak Performance, and Flow: A Comparative Analysis of Positive Human Experiences. *Journal of Personality and Social Psychology, 45*(6), 1361–1368.

Prophet. (2019). Brand Relevance Index. Retrieved from https://www.prophet.com/relevantbrands-2019/.

Puto, C. P., & Wells, W. D. (1984). Informational and Transformational Advertising: The differential Effects of Time. *Advances in Consumer Research, 11*(1), 638–643.

Rapier, G. (2019). Tesla's Reputation with Consumers Took a Big Hit After a Wild Year, According to a New Poll. Retrieved from https://www.businessinsider.com/tesla-reputation-with-consumers-took-big-hit-new-poll-2019-3?r=DE&IR=T.

Rauschnabel, P., Felix, R., & Hinsch, C. (2019). Augmented Reality Marketing: How Mobile AR-Apps Can Improve Brands Through Inspiration. *Journal of Retailing and Consumer Services, 49*, 43–53.

Reber, R., & Greifeneder, R. (2017). Processing Fluency in Education: How Metacognitive Feelings Shape Learning, Belief Formation, and Affect. *Educational Psychologist, 52*(2), 84–103.

Reinartz, W., & Kumar, V. (2000). On the Profitability of Long-Life Customers in a Noncontractual Setting: An Empirical Investigation and Implications for Marketing. *Journal of Marketing, 64*, 17–35.

Reker, G. (2000). Theoretical Perspective, Dimensions, and Measurement of Existential Meaning. In G. T. Reker & K. Chamberlain (Eds.), *Exploring Existential Meaning: Optimizing Human Development across the Life Span* (pp. 39–58). Thousand Oaks: Sage Publications.

Ringle, C. M., Sarstedt, M., & Straub, D. W. (2012). A Critical Look at the Use of PLS-SEM in "MIS Quarterly". *MIS Quarterly, 36*(1), iii-xiv.

Ringle, C. M., Wende, S., & Becker, J.-M. (2015). SmartPLS 3. Retrieved from http://www.smartpls.com.

Rook, D. W., & Fisher, R. J. (1995). Normative Influences on Impulsive Buying Behavior. *Journal of Consumer Research, 22*(3), 305–313.

Rossi, F., & Chintagunta, P. K. (2016). Price Transparency and Retail Prices: Evidence from Fuel Price Signs in the Italian Highway System. *Journal of Marketing Research (JMR), 53*(3), 407–423.

Rossiter, J. R. (2002). The C-OAR-SE Procedure for Scale Development in Marketing. *International Journal of Research in Marketing, 19*(4), 305–335.

Rossiter, J. R. (2011). Marketing Measurement Revolution: The C-OAR-SE Method and Why It Must Replace Psychometrics. *European Journal of Marketing, 45*(11/12), 1561–1588.

Rossiter, J. R. (2012). A New C-OAR-SE-based Content-Valid and Predictively Valid Measure that Distinguishes brand Love from Brand Liking. *Marketing Letters, 23*(3), 905–916.

Rossiter, J. R. (2014). 'Branding' Explained: Defining and Measuring Brand Awareness and Brand Attitude. *Journal of Brand Management, 21*(7/8), 533–540.

Rossiter, J. R., & Percy, L. (1985). Advertising Communication Models. *Advances in Consumer Research, 12*(1), 510–524.

Rudolph, T., & Pfrang, T. (2014). Der Point of Sale als Inspirationsquelle: Kundeninspiration als Markenstrategie. *Planung & Analyse: Zeitschrift für Marktforschung und Marketing, 3*, 28–31.

Rudolph, T., Böttger, T., & Pfrang, T. (2012). Kundeninspiration als Chance für den Handel. *Marketing Review St. Gallen, 29*(5), 8–15.

Rudolph, T., Böttger, T., Pfrang, T., & Evanschitzky, H. (2015). *Customer Inspiration: Conceptualization, Scale Development, and Validation.* Paper presented at the AMA Winter Marketing Educators' Conference 2015, San Antonio, USA.

Rudolph, T., Nagengast, L., & Weber, M. (2014). *Profilierung und Kundeninspiration: Wachstum in Umkämpften Märkten.* St. Gallen: Universität St. Gallen.

Ryan, R. M., & Deci, E. L. (2000). Self-Determination Theory and the Facilitation of Intrinsic Motivation, Social Development, and Well-Being. *American Psychologist, 55*(1), 68–78.

Sabatier, P. A. (1986). Top-down and Bottom-up Approaches to Implementation Research: A Critical Analysis and Suggested Synthesis. *Journal of Public Policy, 6*(1), 21–48.

Sarstedt, M., & Mooi, E. (2014). *A Concise Guide to Market Research: The Process, Data, and Methods Using IBM SPSS Statistics.* New York: Springer.

Sarstedt, M., Hair, J., Hwa, C., Becker, J.-M., & Ringle, C. (2019). How to Specify, Estimate, and Validate Higher-order Constructs in PLS-SEM. *Australasian Marketing Journal, 27*(3), 197–211.

Sarstedt, M., Ringle, C., & Hair, J. F. (2017). Partial Least Squares Structural Equation Modeling. In K. M. Homburg C., Vomberg A. (Ed.), *Handbook of Market Research.* Cham: Springer.

Schermelleh-Engel, K., Moosbrugger, H., & Müller, H. (2003). Evaluating the Fit of Structural Equation Models: Tests of Significance and Descriptive Goodness-of-Fit Measures. *Methods of Psychological Research Online, 8*(8), 23–74.

Schivinski, B., Christodoulides, G., & Dabrowski, D. (2016). Measuring Consumers' Engagement With Brand-Related Social-Media Content: Development and Validation of a Scale that Identifies Levels of Social-Media Engagement with Brands. *Journal of Advertising Research, 56*(1), 64–80.

Schouten, J. W., & McAlexander, J. H. (1995). Subcultures of Consumption: An Ethnography of the New Bikers. *Journal of Consumer Research, 22*(1), 43–61.

Schouten, J. W., McAiexander, J. H., & Koenig, H. F. (2007). Transcendent Customer Experience and Brand Community. *Journal of the Academy of Marketing Science, 35*(3), 357–368.

Schwaiger, M. (2004). Components and Parameters of Corporate Reputation—An Empirical Study. *Schmalenbach Business Review, 56*(1), 46–71.

Shamir, B., House, R. J., & Arthur, M. B. (1993). The Motivational Effects of Charismatic Leadership: A Self-Concept Based Theory. *Organization Science, 4*(4), 577–594.

Sharp, B. (1995). Brand Equity and Market-Based Assets of Professional Service Firms. *Journal of Professional Services Marketing, 13*(1), 3–13.

Shavitt, S., & Brock, T. C. (1986). Self-Relevant Responses in Commercial Persuasion: Field and Experimental Tests. *Advertising and consumer psychology, 3*, 149–171.

Sheehan, D., & Dommer, S. L. (2020). Saving Your Self: How Identity Relevance Influences Product Usage. *Journal of Consumer Research, 46*(6), 1076–1092.

Sheeran, P. (2002). Intention—Behavior Relations: A Conceptual and Empirical Review. *European Review of Social Psychology, 12*, 1–36.

Shimp, T. A. (1981). Attitude Toward the Ad as a Mediator of Consumer Brand Choice. *Journal of Advertising, 10*(2), 9–48.

Shimp, T. A., & Madden, T. J. (1988). Consumer-Object Relations: A Conceptual Framework Based Analogously on Sternberg's Triangular Theory of Love. *Advances in Consumer Research, 15*(1), 163–168.

Shiota, M. N., Thrash, T. M., Danvers, A. F., & Dombrowski, J. T. (2014). *Transcending the self: Awe, Elevation, and Inspiration.* New York: The Guilford Press.

Shmueli, G. (2011). To Explain or to Predict? *Statistical Science, 25*(3), 289–310.

Shmueli, G., Sarstedt, M., Hair, J., Hwa, C., Ting, H., Vaithilingam, S., & Ringle, C. (2019). Predictive Model Assessment in PLS-SEM: Guidelines for Using PLSpredict. *European Journal of Marketing, 53*(11), 2322–2347.

Siemens Home. (2020). Inspiration. Retrieved from https://www.siemens-home.bsh-group. com/de/inspiration/inspiration.

Sinek, S. (2011). *Start With Why.* Harlow: Penguin Books.

Skaar, Ø. O., & Reber, R. (2020). The Phenomenology of Aha-Experiences. *Motivation Science, 6*(1), 49–60.

Smith, R. E., & Wright, W. F. (2004). Determinants of Customer Loyalty and Financial Performance. *Journal of Management Accounting Research, 16*, 183–205.

So, K. K. F., King, C., & Sparks, B. (2012). Customer Engagement With Tourism Brands: Scale Development and Validation. *Journal of Hospitality and Tourism Research, 38*(3), 304–329.

Spears, N., & Singh, S. (2004). Measuring Attitude Toward the Brand and Purchase Intentions. *Journal of Current Issues and Research in Advertising, 26*(2), 53–66.

Stahl, F., Heitmann, M., Lehmann, D. R., & Neslin, S. A. (2012). The Impact of Brand Equity on Customer Acquisition, Retention, and Profit Margin. *Journal of Marketing, 76*(4), 44–63.

Steenkamp, J.-B. E. M., Van Heerde, H. J., & Geyskens, I. (2010). What Makes Consumers Willing to Pay a Price Premium for National Brands over Private Labels? *Journal of Marketing Research, 47*(6), 1011–1024.

Stephan, E., Sedikides, C., Wildschut, T., Cheung, W.-Y., Routledge, C., & Arndt, J. (2015). Nostalgia-Evoked Inspiration: Mediating Mechanisms and Motivational Implications. *Personality and Social Psychology Bulletin, 41*(10), 1395–1410.

Stokburger-Sauer, N., Ratneshwar, S., & Sen, S. (2012). Drivers of Consumer–Brand Identification. *International Journal of Research in Marketing, 29*(4), 406–418.

Strauss, A., & Corbin, J. M. (1990). *Basics of Qualitative Research: Grounded Theory Procedures and Techniques.* Thousand Oaks: Sage Publications.

Swaminathan, V., Sorescu, A., Steenkamp, J.-B. E. M., O'Guinn, T. C. G., & Schmitt, B. (2020). Branding in a Hyperconnected World: Refocusing Theories and Rethinking Boundaries. *Journal of Marketing, 84*(2), 24–46.

Tajfel, H., & Turner, J. (2004). The Social Identity Theory of Intergroup Behavior: Key Readings. In J. T. Jost & J. Sidanius (Eds.), *Key Readings in Social Psychology. Political Psychology: Key Readings* (pp. 276–293). Hove: Psychology Press.

Tassimo. (2020). Inspiration. Retrieved from https://www.tassimo.com/de/inspiration.

Tellis, G. J., MacInnis, D. J., Tirunillai, S., & Zhang, Y. (2019). What Drives Virality (Sharing) of Online Digital Content? The Critical Role of Information, Emotion, and Brand Prominence. *Journal of Marketing, 83*(4), 1–20.

Tesla. (2020). Imagine. Retrieved from https://www.youtube.com/watch?v=OU368Y gQb-M.

Thompson, C. J., Rindfleisch, A., & Arsel, Z. (2006). Emotional Branding and the Strategic Value of the Doppelgänger Brand Image. *Journal of Marketing, 70*(1), 50–64.

Thomson, M., MacInnis, D. J., & Park, C. W. (2005). The Ties That Bind: Measuring the Strength of Consumers' Emotional Attachments to Brands. *Journal of Consumer Psychology, 15*(1), 77–91.

Thrash, T. M., & Elliot, A. J. (2003). Inspiration as a Psychological Construct. *Journal of Personality and Social Psychology, 84*(4), 871–889.

Thrash, T. M., & Elliot, A. J. (2004). Inspiration: Core Characteristics, Component Processes, Antecedents, and Function. *Journal of Personality and Social Psychology, 87*(6), 957–973.

Thrash, T. M., Elliot, A. J., Maruskin, L. A., & Cassidy, S. E. (2010a). Inspiration and the Promotion of Well-Being: Tests of Causality and Mediation. *Journal of Personality and Social Psychology, 98*(3), 488–506.

Thrash, T. M., Maruskin, L. A., Cassidy, S. E., Fryer, J. W., & Ryan, R. M. (2010). Mediating Between the Muse and the Masses: Inspiration and the Actualization of Creative Ideas. *Journal of Personality and Social Psychology, 98*(3), 469–487.

Thrash, T. M., Maruskin, L. A., Moldovan, E. G., Oleynick, V. C., & Belzak, W. C. (2017). Writer–Reader Contagion of Inspiration and Related States: Conditional Process Analyses within a Cross-Classified Writer × Reader Framework. *Journal of Personality and Social Psychology, 113*(3), 466–491.

Topolinski, S., & Reber, R. (2010). Gaining Insight Into the "Aha" Experience. *Current directions in Psychological Science, 19*(6), 402–405.

Tucker, C. E. (2015). The Reach and Persuasiveness of Viral Video Ads. *Marketing Science, 34*(2), 281–296.

Udell, J. G. (1965). Can Attitude Measurement Predict Consumer Behavior? *Journal of Marketing, 29*(4), 46–50.

Umashankar, N., Bhagwat, Y., & Kumar, V. (2017). Do Loyal Customers Really Pay More for Services? *Journal of the Academy of Marketing Science, 45*(6), 807–826.

Umashankar, N., Ward, M. K., & Dahl, D. W. (2017). The Benefit of Becoming Friends: Complaining After Service Failures Leads Customers with Strong Ties to Increase Loyalty. *Journal of Marketing, 81*(6), 79–98.

Vakratsas, D., & Ambler, T. (1999). How Advertising Works: What Do We Really Know? *Journal of Marketing, 63*(1), 26–43.

Van Doorn, J., Lemon, K. N., Mittal, V., Nass, S., Pick, D., Pirner, P., & Verhoef, P. C. (2010). Customer Engagement Behavior: Theoretical Foundations and Research Directions. *Journal of Service Research, 13*(3), 253–266.

van Zalk, M. H. W., Nestler, S., Geukes, K., Hutteman, R., & Back, M. D. (2020). The Codevelopment of Extraversion and Friendships: Bonding and Behavioral Interaction Mechanisms in Friendship Networks. *Journal of Personality and Social Psychology, 118*(6), 1269–1290.

Vence, D. L. (2005). Work the Room. *Marketing News, 39*(4), 49–51.

Verhoef, P. C. (2003). Understanding the Effect of Customer Relationship Management Efforts on Customer Retention and Customer Share Development. *Journal of Marketing, 67*(4), 30–45.

Vivek, S. (2009). *A Scale of Consumer Engagement.* (Dissertation), The University of Alabama Alabama, US.

Vivek, S., Beatty, S. E., & Morgan, R. (2012). Customer Engagement: Exploring Customer Relationships Beyond Purchase. *Journal of Marketing Theory and Practice, 20*(2), 127–145.

Vivek, S., Beatty, S. E., Dalela, V., & Morgan, R. M. (2014). A Generalized Multidimensional Scale for Measuring Customer Engagement. *Journal of Marketing Theory & Practice, 22*(4), 401–420.

Wanous, J. P., & Reichers, A. E. (1996). Estimating the Reliability of a Single-Item Measure. *78*(2), 631–634.

Warren, C., Batra, R., Loureiro, S. M. C., & Bagozzi, R. P. (2019). Brand Coolness. *Journal of Marketing, 83*(5), 36–56.

Watson, D., Clark, L. A., & Tellegen, A. (1988). Development and Validation of Brief Measures of Positive and Negative Affect: The PANAS Scales. *Journal of Personality and Social Psychology, 54*(6), 1063–1070.

Watson, G., Beck, J., Henderson, C., & Palmatier, R. (2015). Building, Measuring, and Profiting from Customer Loyalty. *Journal of the Academy of Marketing Science, 43*(6), 790–825.

Weisberg, D. (2014). The Development of Imaginative Cognition. *Royal Institute of Philosophy Supplement, 75*, 85–103.

Williams, M. H. (1982). *Inspiration in Milton and Keats.* London: Macmillian.

Winklhofer, H. M., & Diamantopoulos, A. (2002). Managerial Evaluation of Sales Forecasting Effectiveness: A MIMIC Modeling Approach. *International Journal of Research in Marketing, 19*(2), 151–166.

Winterich, K. P., Nenkov, G. Y., & Gonzales, G. E. (2019). Knowing What It Makes: How Product Transformation Salience Increases Recycling. *Journal of Marketing, 83*(4), 21–37.

Wirtz, B. W. (2001). *Electronic Business* (2nd ed.). Wiesbaden: Gabler Verlag.

Wood, L. (2000). Brands and Brand Equity: Definition and Management. *Management Decision, 38*(9), 662–669.

Yim, C. K., Tse, D. K., & Chan, K. W. (2008). Strengthening Customer Loyalty Through Intimacy and Passion: Roles of Customer–Firm Affection and Customer–Staff Relationships in Services. *Journal of Marketing Research, 45*(6), 741–756.

Yoo, C., & MacInnis, D. (2005). The Brand Attitude Formation Process of Emotional and Informational Ads. *Journal of Business Research, 58*(10), 1397–1406.

Yu, T., Patterson, P., & de Ruyter, K. (2015). Converting Service Encounters into Cross-Selling Opportunities: Does Faith in Supervisor Ability Help or Hinder Service-Sales Ambidexterity? *European Journal of Marketing, 49*(3/4), 491–511.

Yukl, G. A. (1998). *Leadership in Organizations.* Upper Saddle River: Prentice Hall.

Yuwei, J., Adaval, R., Steinhart, Y., & Wyer Jr, R. S. (2014). Imagining Yourself in the Scene: The Interactive Effects of Goal-Driven Self- Imagery and Visual Perspectives on Consumer Behavior. *Journal of Consumer Research, 41*(2), 418–435.

Zaichkowsky, J. (1985). Measuring the Involvement Construct. *Journal of Consumer Research, 12*(3), 341–352.

Zaltman, G., Lemasters, K., & Heffring, M. (1982). *Theory Construction in Marketing: Some Thoughts on Thinking.* New York: John Wiley & Sons.

Zeithaml, V. A., Jaworski, B. J., Kohli, A. K., Tuli, K. R., Ulaga, W., & Zaltman, G. (2020). A Theories-in-Use Approach to Building Marketing Theory. *Journal of Marketing, 84*(1), 32–51.

Zinnbauer, M., & Eberl, M. (2005). Überprüfung der Spezifikation und Güte von Struktur-gleichungsmodellen. *WiSt—Wirtschaftswissenschaftliches Studium, 34*(10), 566–572.

Zuckerman, M. (1983). The Distinction between Trait and State Scales is not Arbitrary: Comment on Allen and Potkay's 'On the Arbitrary Distinction between Traits and States'. *Journal of Personality and Social Psychology, 44*(5), 1083–1086.

CPSIA information can be obtained
at www.ICGtesting.com
Printed in the USA
LVHW011247151121
703346LV00001B/127